D1458713

The God Who
Speaks

The God Who Speaks

IAN PETIT OSB

daybreak

London

First published in 1989 by
Daybreak
Darton, Longman and Todd Ltd
1 Spencer Court
140–142 Wandsworth High Street
London SW18 4JJ

Reprinted 1991 and 1992

British Library Cataloguing in Publication Data

Petit, Ian
    The God who speaks
    1. Christian life. Faith
    I. Title
    248.4

    ISBN 0–232–51802–5

The publishers would like to thank McCrimmon
Publishing Co. Ltd for permission to quote from the
author's contribution to *Anointed with the Spirit* 1978, in
the introduction to this book.

Phototypeset by Input Typesetting Ltd,
London SW19 8DR
Printed and bound in Great Britain by
Page Bros, Norwich

Contents

Preface

I wonder if we are right in imagining that every Christian has been evangelised? The gospel message is far-ranging, and it is possible to get attached to our own part of it and miss the central point. So much depends on how we were introduced to it. From my experience of counselling, I have discovered that many of us have built our religion on secondary truths, and although the central truth has never been denied, it has never become a living force in our lives.

I see this as a serious sickness in the Church, because if Christianity is not experienced as life-giving, then either we heroically embrace something which is not the gospel or we abandon religion. You cannot put your faith in what you do not know, and when there is no faith in what God has done through the death and rising of his Son, then can we honestly say there is new life?

In this book I want to spell out in very simple language the central truth of the gospel. The trouble with stating profound truths simply is that it leaves much unsaid, so misunderstandings can arise. But then accuracy can also have its problems, because in the desire to be exact subclause gets added to subclause, and clarity is sacrificed in the quest for precision.

I, who had the advantage of studying some theology, managed to miss the central point of the gospel, so what of those who have not had that advantage? I do not blame my teachers, but I do blame that image I had of God long before I opened any theology book. That is why I want to go back to basics and spell out the foundations.

I write for those who honestly recognise their difficulty in understanding and living out the gospel, and for those who plod along with only a very hazy comprehension. I also write for those who have set out on the Christian way but become disenchanted and given up, and for others who are not from a Christian background and who may know little about the gospel.

We are all pilgrims, we are all on a journey. Most of this book is my travelogue. I offer it in the hope that it might help others on their journey.

IAN PETIT OSB

Introduction

I have to confess that I only really began to understand the central truths of the gospel after I had been a priest for many years. The crucial time of enlightenment for me came at the end of the 1960s and in the early 1970s.

I had been one of a team of four monks who had been sent out in 1956 from Ampleforth Abbey in Yorkshire to St Louis, Missouri, USA. Our task was to found a monastery and a school. The years there had been very demanding and from about 1967 onwards I was at a very low ebb both physically and spiritually. Weariness and overwork can bring about a spiritual crisis. I was heading for some of the roughest years of my life. It was not just dryness; I was on the verge of complete disillusionment. I had given my all, left home and country, worked till fit to drop; and here I was empty, tired, and even questioning the principles I had held as gospel truth. I cannot pretend that the insights brought about by Vatican II helped me much; they only confirmed in me that there was something very amiss in the way I had picked up religion and monasticism.

Quite close to our Priory, there was a Visitation convent. I was one of their confessors and I often gave them spiritual conferences. In August 1968, just after I had come back from my summer holidays, they phoned me to say they had had some exciting talks on prayer given by the Dominican, Fr Francis MacNutt, and a Baptist minister. When I went down to see them, I confess I could not understand what they were talking about. I heard about the Holy Spirit, the gift of tongues, the gifts of the Spirit, the Good News of the gospel. I did not know what all the excitement was about – it certainly was not my present experience, and I was highly suspicious of all this enthusiasm. Surely religion was meant to be much pain and struggle?

For a year I attended their prayer meetings. I had a love-hate relationship with all I saw going on. I certainly needed help, and I wanted all this love, joy and peace, but there was much that turned me off. Fortunately, I saw that my hesitancy was due to cultural rather than theological reasons. But I have to admit I was very suspicious of these Protestant people.

In August 1969, health intervened, I lost weight rapidly, exhaustion was diagnosed and that October I was packed off home to Europe for the rest of the year. I did not want to go – being busy can stop you from thinking a thing through; now I would have time, and I might

2

think myself not only out of the priesthood, but even out of Christianity.

I rapidly recovered my physical health, though sleep was a problem. I travelled much, rested, walked, but spiritually I seemed to have died. I could not pray, and I seemed quite incapable of communicating my desolation to anyone. It is virtually impossible to explain what a priest in crisis feels like; after all, you are meant to be an expert in spiritual matters, so people do not expect you ever to have a crisis in that realm.

At the end of the year, it was suggested I should stay longer, but I felt I could not spend my life resting. It was decided that I should return to St Louis, although I was not to take up my teaching yet.

On my return, of course, I went down to the Visitation convent. There they were, all praising God; and the fascination rose up in me again. How those sisters had grown! It was then that I heard about Pecos – a Benedictine Priory that had gone charismatic. Benedictines would be safe; so off I went down there.

I talked with Fr David Geraets, who has since become their abbot, and I told him I had read everything I could lay my hands on, I had attended many prayer meetings, but I could not experience any of this peace they all talked about. I had even begun to wonder if I was damned or possessed. He alarmed me by asking me if I had ever spoken in tongues. I told him

3

that I had a real problem with 'tongues' – why should an intelligent God want an intelligent creature to pray to him in an unintelligible way? He explained that it was sometimes necessary to do something we could not understand, because with priests and ministers we run the danger of having only intellectual faith. We know answers; and we think we believe because we can give an answer. He suggested that launching out into tongues would be a real act of faith for me. So I explained, with much embarrassment, that as a small boy I had often pretended that I was a foreigner and I would jabber on the buses in London with my brothers and sisters. I have a good ear and I can imitate French, Spanish and Italian sounds, even Oriental noises! I must confess I thought that that would floor him. But not at all! 'Oh, you are lucky,' he replied. 'You've got the mechanics. All you have to do, is to submit that to God.' I could not accept that.

That afternoon I went for a walk in the mountains surrounding the Priory. It was a windy day and the clouds were fast moving and low. I can remember standing there in the hills shaking my fist at heaven. 'Why don't you speak? Do you have to drive a man mad before you will answer?' I was angry; but nothing happened – no parting of the clouds, no light. That night after compline, several people staying at the Priory asked to be prayed over. I had seen this happen many times, I had often

4

stood in the circle and had even prayed aloud. This time as we were praying, I heard one monk praying in tongues quite softly. I felt, 'I might as well try this out. I'll go to the end of this branch to see if anything is there'. So, in cold deliberation I committed my voice to God and did my party-piece. Nothing happened. The people we prayed for looked more dead than any people we had prayed for before; but more important to me, nothing happened in me. So that was the end; I was grateful none of my own brethren had been present to see me make a fool of myself.

Next morning I awoke feeling very foolish. While waiting for morning office to begin, I pulled out my New Testament and opened it at random. My eyes fell on the text: 'Go, I am sending you far away to the Gentiles.' I do not think I really understood the text, but it was as though I heard someone say those words right down inside me as I read them. You must understand that after almost two years of nearly total silence, this was a profound moment. I remember closing the book in a hurry and saying, 'That is for St Paul. Not me'. But something had happened.

That day I listened to talks being given to the retreatants, and the message was very simple and clear. 'I want men of faith in my Church. I do not want men who know everything. I want men who will believe in me, who will do what I say. Even walk on water if I should command them.' Did all this happen because of this 'talking in tongues'? Was it really 'talking in tongues'? I do not know the answers to these questions; all I know is something changed. I felt compelled to go on exploring.

A few months later, I was at Ann Arbor. I met there a Fr George Kosicki CSB. He told me that he was starting a small house of prayer for priests, where we could honestly ask all the questions we wanted, where we could search together into this renewal. I told him I was his first candidate. So having gone up to Ann Arbor for a weekend, I actually stayed up in the Detroit area for nearly five months. The experience was not easy. I was living with a group of people who expected things to happen. Things did happen but I was suspicious that we read more into the happenings than was there. I feared the text in Scripture referring to those who did great things in the name of Christ but in the end even Jesus claimed not to know them. But one thing made me stay – I have never experienced such love. I had every argument against them and what they honestly stood for, but they never grew impatient with me and were very loving. This must be of God.

After three months or more I had to confess to Fr George that really inside me I was still lost. I had learnt much, I could pray aloud, I could raise my arms without too much embarrassment, I even sang in tongues when the group praised in that way – but I could not honestly say with conviction 'Alleluia'. George asked me if I was still using the gift of tongues. I told him that I joined in the singing when the group did. But he said, 'No, you should use it in your own personal, private prayer. You had an experience with the gift, you must now consciously use it.' So I began for a few minutes each day doing what he told me. On the third day, when I had just finished doing this, and I was turning round to come back to the house, I suddenly understood the gospel: 'Why are you so full of fear? Why are you always trying to win my favour? Can you not see I have sent you my Son and he has reconciled you. I want you to live in him and live as son.' I did not hear these words, it was as though I spoke them to myself within myself. But now I had come to understand. I was through the wall; I saw the Good News, understood at last what it meant to be in Christ Jesus.

Looking back on those years of personal trauma, I can now see a meaning in them, although at the time it was not at all clear what was happening and I imagined that I was on my way out of the priesthood and even of the Church. I am amazed to think, after all my theological and scriptural training, that I had such a wrong understanding of the gospel. I know now that God had to deal with this misunderstanding but I fought tooth and nail against his reordering of my thoughts, fearing that I was being tempted to doubt and abandon the very foundation on which my spiritual life had been built. I now see that that very foundation had to be destroyed. It was not that my theological training was wrong; what was wrong was the base on which it rested. God, for me, was someone to fear, someone I had to placate, humour, and I shaped everything I learnt to fit in with this misconception. God had to break the stranglehold my wrong picture of him had over me, but as he did this, I imagined that my faith was being shattered, when all the time he was shattering the bogey that I thought was God.

I have written this book to share something of the fruit of that crisis in my life. My new understanding did not come in flashing revelations – indeed it has been a long and often painful journey into light. But I thank God for it now, as I am able to comprehend how the gospel can appear anything but life-giving for some people. I understand how people can listen to the gospel and not see it as the solution. My life was not wicked, nor peppered with great sins, but it was full of *my* directing, *my* efforts, *my* making myself holy. I needed to learn that that sort of life has been dealt with by Christ's dying and rising. That is what this book is about. It is not a testimony, though I do share much of my own experience; nor is it a book about the charismatic renewal, and speaking in tongues. Rather I am trying to show how basic misconceptions can persist in spite of sound teaching. So, as you read, be honest with yourself and admit your basic feelings and ideas about God. These may have to surface into the light, but as we confess our wrong ideas and attitudes, the Spirit of God brings about the forgiveness and healing that Jesus won for us at such great cost.

1

Beyond Ourselves

Since the Spirit is our life, let us be directed by the Spirit. (Gal. 5:26)

I cannot remember my first thoughts of God or when I was first told about him. I came from a Catholic family, so very early on I would have heard about God, and I would have been taken to church at a young age. Somewhere along the line, I picked up the idea that God was not someone I was too keen to know. I heard that he knew everything, and I found that disconcerting for it meant I had no secrets from him. I was told he was good, and that was uncomfortable because I was *not* good; it was not that I was wicked, but I certainly was not good. How deep first impressions must go for surely I must have heard that God loved me, but that did not seem to erase my conviction that he was someone to fear. I do not know who communicated that fear to me – I am sure no one taught it directly. I must have picked up many different impressions and built them into a picture. From my own experience of trying to teach others about God, I realise how very difficult it is to communicate the truth; it is so easy to make God too hard or too soft, but how very important those early communications are.

From these first, rather negative impressions other ideas grew. The stories from the Old Testament did not improve the picture, but rather confirmed the notion that this God was not to be meddled with. I found church services boring, as I suppose most children do, and slowly, without actually saying it in so many words, I concluded that God was a bit of a spoil-sport frowning on anything that was enjoyable and promoting anything that hurt or was dull.

I would not say I was an irreligious child. Put me under a beech tree just after its leaves had come out, show me a sunset or a magnificent view and my spirit would soar. I could stay for hours just staring at the beauty of nature – a clear sky washed clean by the rain, a wild seascape, an autumn wood. I do not think it was just sensuous; deep down I felt I was in contact with something, or someone, sacred. I found poetry had the same effect on me, and when I heard about the great god Pan I half wondered if I had met him in the woods; and I grew fearful in case this is what the Gospels meant when they talked about 'loving the world'. All this set up a strange tension in me, for I could see no connection between what I

11

was finding in the fields and what I learnt about in church. In fact, it has taken most of my life to bring these two together, and the marriage is still fairly fragile – first impressions do die hard.

I believe it was my spirit that was being touched at those moments when I seemed to be drawn out of myself and in touch with something 'other'. It is strange that my religion which should have been all about the spirit never touched me in that way but just brought fear and dread. Later the sense of mystery did appear but it was always mixed with anxiety. We all have a spirit and it would be good if you could try to see how your spirit may have made itself known to you. Most of us experience sudden questions that rise up from apparently nowhere: 'What is it all for? Where am I going?' These questions are uncomfortable and we can dismiss them and fail to respond to a moment of grace. There are other times when we seem to be taken out of ourselves, as though we were lifted up above our life and see things from a different perspective. It may be when walking in nature, or listening to music, or reading poetry; for each of us it will be different. We cannot make this sort of thing happen; they are moments of grace and we should learn to welcome these ambassadors from the land deep within ourselves. Too often we let our false pictures of God inhibit us and we ignore the promptings of our spirit. Or perhaps we are suspicious of such promptings because we are afraid our friends might laugh at us if we share them. We find it so difficult to trust our own experience of God and frequently listen to the voice of authority or of others rather than listen to what God is saying to us through our spirit.

Body, soul and spirit

We are more than just body and soul; we are body, soul and *spirit*. For years I thought my soul *was* my spirit, and it was only after someone had pointed out to me the passage in Hebrews where it says that the word of God 'can slip through the place where the soul is divided from the spirit' (4:12) that I began to be aware of this separation of soul and spirit. Every time I met the word 'spirit' in Scripture I paid special attention and I began to see that there was a whole way of knowing that did not involve the reasoning process. With my mind, I can come to conclusions through a process of deductive thinking and I can explain afterwards just how I reached those conclusions. But when I know something in my spirit, I cannot say how I know; all I know is, I know.

Our thought process is very complex. Truths are conveyed to us through ideas and reasoning. But these are limited and cannot fully contain or convey the reality they wish to express. There is a reality that lies beyond words and cannot be reached by words, thoughts or ideas.

I understand revelation to be when God imparts a truth without me having to go through a process of deduction. I cannot make this happen, but I can allow stillness to be part of my life, so that when the small voice of God speaks, in my stillness I will be able to hear it.

I think at this point I should attempt a brief definition of body, soul and spirit. I do so hesitantly as I realise how difficult it is to describe adequately the make-up of a human being, but some sort of definition is needed. Through the body we are 'physical' beings and partake in the material world. Through the soul we are 'rational' beings, able to live in the immaterial as well as the material world and bringing into play our reason, our will, our imagination and our emotions. Through the spirit we are 'spiritual' beings and operate in a realm beyond the reach of body and soul. It is through our spirit that God communicates with us and that we receive the gift of the Holy Spirit; intuition and inspiration are important here.

It might be helpful to use the word 'heart' in place of spirit, but I am a little reluctant to do so as the word 'heart' is often identified with feeling, emotion, sentiment as when someone says, 'he touched my heart'. There is another sense for the word 'heart' as when we say, 'my heart is not in it' or 'in my heart I feel that is wrong': here my inmost being is in question and that is what I want to call my spirit. The best example I know which shows someone

14

coming to knowledge through the spirit is Peter's declaration that Jesus is the Christ, the Son of the living God; look at Jesus' response to Peter: 'Blessed are you, Simon son of Jonah, you are a happy man! Because it was not flesh and blood that revealed this to you but my Father in heaven' (Matt. 16:17). Peter had not come to this truth through any rational process ('flesh and blood') but because the Father had revealed it to him.

In the western world much effort has been spent on developing our bodies and souls, but because of the vague ideas we have about spirit, we have not developed that side of ourselves to the same extent. We are suspicious of inspiration – we are factual, practical and logical people. But since God communicates himself to us through our spirit, how important it is that we develop our spiritual side. The need to learn about the realm of the spirit is all the more pressing because of the growing interest in the occult and the current fascination with Eastern mysticism; many people, disenchanted with materialism, are turning to the world of the spirit, and it is essential for Christians to be familiar with this world. This does not mean that we are to ignore our body and soul; these are to be developed as well although not to the neglect of our spirit. We will look at how we can nurture our spirit in more detail later. First of all let us look at things with which we are more familiar: our body and soul. As we do this, we must avoid putting ourselves into compartments; we are one person who can operate in three different spheres.

Through our body we are privileged to be part of the material world. Some people imagine that to be spiritual entails rising above the body and escaping into a rarefied atmosphere of the spirit. God made the world of matter and he saw and declared it was good; so it must not be spurned. Think what it means to be able to touch and feel, to put things together and take them apart. What a wonderful thing colour is – how dull it would be to see everything as a black and white photograph. Angels cannot see, touch, hear or smell. They have no contact with the material world as we do. God's plan was that we should be part of this material universe, so he fashioned us from the very dust of the earth.

Try to think of some of the things you particularly like doing; it may be playing a sport, walking in the countryside, cooking a meal, doing embroidery – all such things are to be enjoyed and we should not despise them. I can remember the first time I learnt to water-ski. I am a sun lover, and when I was sent to be part of a monastic foundation in the United States, it was an extraordinary experience to see so much blue sky and to find the sun was actually too hot. I learnt to water-ski in Michigan. It all happened on one of those glorious summer days that one thought only existed in holiday brochures. Everything was sparkling, the lake was warm and the sky was a sharp, deep blue. Being something of an athlete and having had experience on roller and ice-skates, to everyone's amazement, I managed to get up on the skis straightaway. What a sensation it was to fizz across the top of that blue lake with cool spray splashing all over my body. One might say that it was all very sensuous, but in some way I felt that I had touched God, or, more amazingly, that he had touched me. It is hard to describe what a profound effect that experience had on me; having felt God's touch there, I began to see his touch was always present, hidden in less spectacular moments. Thus through bodily pleasures God is able to speak to our spirit, and, as I said earlier, we should be careful not to put ourselves into compartments and to separate rigidly our experiences into those of the body, those of the soul and those of the spirit.

When Genesis tells us that God created the human race, there seems to be a change in his way of creating. Instead of just saying, 'Let there be man', he says: 'Let us make man in our own image, in the likeness of ourselves and let them be masters of the fish of the sea, the birds of heaven, the cattle, all the wild beasts and all the reptiles that crawl upon the earth' (1:26). It seems as though there was a committee meeting in the Godhead over the creation of this all-important creature. We were

17

to be masters over the world of matter and in order for this to happen we needed to be more than body: we needed an intelligence.

So we are not just to be *part* of the material world; we are to be *masters* of it, and for this we need to be able to know it and understand it – we need to bring our soul into operation. What an extraordinary thing it is to know something; not just to see it, but to know and recognise it for what it is. Through our observance of the world around us, we have been able to see that things do not just happen, and we have discovered that matter is subject to laws. We are not always able to trace exactly why certain things happen; all we can say is they have a nature which makes them act or react in a certain way. When God made the world he did not make it complete and fully developed. He planned to have his world explored and developed by the creatures he chose to be its masters. What ingenious creatures we are; just a simple glance at what we have achieved is indeed staggering. We have learnt to fly, and that at great speed; we can talk to people on the other side of the world, and we can even see what they are doing at the moment they do it; we have put men on the moon and brought them back again.

Not only are we able to draw knowledge and insights from the material world around us, but we can also enter the immaterial world of abstract ideas. Our thinking is not confined to what we can imagine; we can also deal with abstract ideas – we can juggle with concepts and draw conclusions after complex processes of deduction. So our thinking is not limited to the material world; we can explore the world of ideas. We are like unto God in that we are reasoning beings. In giving us a soul, God gave us power to reason, to remember, to experience emotion and to decide on a course of action. We were not called to be robots doing the will of God automatically. God gave us the incredible privilege of being responsible creatures. Free will is not the liberty to do what we want; it is the liberty to do willingly what we were created for.

As with our body, I think it would be good if you could consider the ways in which you take pleasure in the gifts of the soul; for example some of us are very imaginative and enjoy the riches our imaginations can offer; others of us take satisfaction in solving problems and thinking things through logically; and still others are able to grapple with complex, abstract ideas. At school I never seemed to shine at my studies – my gifts were athletic. So when I began to teach I felt very much at one with students who said they did not understand the lessons. I knew the misery of not knowing what masters were talking about, and dreading that this would be exposed by my being asked a question. School life did have its special agonies, and so I became very

inventive in trying to show slow students that
they could cope with these intellectual gymnas-
tics. It was a long process but what joy there
was when one day their eyes lit up and they
said: 'Now I see; now I've got it.' Twenty years
further on, it is marvellous to meet some of
these 'slow' students and to see what fine,
competent and capable young men they have
grown into.

Even though our soul can deal with abstract
ideas and the immaterial, it is unable to reach
the world of spirit. We can grapple with spiritual concepts and speculate about them, but the
world of spirit is beyond our soul. Hence God
also made us spirit so that he could communicate his will to us, and have us ponder that
communication and work out how to put it into
action, and finally call our whole being into
operation. The human being is God's prize
creation. We are not just pure animal, nor just
pure intelligence, nor just pure spirit. We
partake in all three worlds and we are called to
a harmonious unity of spirit, soul and body –
in that order. We are not to lose our earthiness,
nor our brilliance, nor the power to walk in the
cool of the evening with the One who made us.

It is fairly obvious when we are operating in
our body. When we see, touch or hear things,
we use our body. It is interesting to note that
we do not say 'My eyes see' or 'My nose smells',
but 'I see', 'I smell' – we identify ourselves
with our body. When we operate in our soul,

understanding how we act is not such a simple matter. Clearly, I can decide to think about someone, but actually what I do to make that happen is not very easy to describe. You, surely, have had the experience of trying to remember something which seems just out of reach of your mind. We often say: 'It is on the tip of my tongue.' Try describing what you do when you try to remember; it is difficult to explain how you do it. It is not like looking for the car keys because then you can turn out pockets, search under the cushions of chairs and sort through your desk; but when trying to remember something we do not use any muscles or perform any obvious actions. Yet, we are able to remember. We can understand what it means to think, act, call to mind, have an emotion, but the actual process involved in making these things happen is a very baffling one. So, trying to describe how our soul actually works is difficult. Because our spirit has been rather neglected, it is even harder to explain what happens when our spirit operates. I suppose most of us have experienced intuition. Somehow we *know* something without being aware of how or even why. It can be a very strong and certain knowledge, and when we discover that it turns out to be true, we say, 'I just knew I was right'. It is an area we are suspicious about, and of course we can be mistaken because not everything in the spiritual world is good and holy; there are evil

21

spirits. Jesus promised to send his Holy Spirit of truth to us. While he was on earth he taught the truth and before he left he promised to send his followers the Spirit of truth to be their continual guide. Spirit speaks to spirit, and it is in our spirit that the Holy Spirit communicates God's word. How necessary it is for us to understand more about our own spirit, but first of all we need to know how our spirit lost its ascendency over our body and soul.

2

Like God but Not God

You have made him a little less than a god.
(Ps. 8:5)

We were made to be *like* God, but not to *be*
God – this is the drama behind the story of the
Fall, and it has ever since remained the drama
for all human life. God endowed human beings
with extraordinary gifts and powers; he made
them in his own image and likeness, and placed
them in authority over the beautiful world he
had created. Alas, they abused their privileged
position, and in rejecting their creaturehood
they made a bid to rival God. The story of the
Fall isn't just about how God's special creatures
went wrong; it is about how those special creatures and all their descendants became
damaged and bent, while remaining exceed-
ingly gifted.

When science looks at creation, it does so
from a scientific point of view. It asks the questions: what? how? and when? The Bible ap-
proaches creation in a different way: it asks
who? and why? There should be no disharmony

between these two disciplines provided each keeps to its own field. Once religion tries to answer scientific questions, then trouble occurs, and the same is true when science enters the realm of religion. So when we read Scripture we must not approach it with a scientific mind. We need to know that the words used often have deep symbolic meanings, and we should avoid getting hung up on words, for, after all, it is the events, not the words, that are important; so we need to search deeply for the inner meaning. That is why we must pray to the Holy Spirit of God and ask him to enlighten our spirits, so that our minds can be flooded with truth. I used to read Scripture trying like mad to understand it, hoping that then I would come to believe it. I now see that I had things upside down – I ought first to believe Scripture and then work like mad to understand it.

I never got very much from the story of creation in Genesis until a friend began to unwrap it for me. I was amazed at how much could be uncovered once I moved beyond the plain meaning of the words. I began to see how much my mind had been influenced by western pragmatic thinking, and I needed to be taught how to think in a new way. Could this be why fairy stories have such an appeal for us? Is there a part of us which is undeveloped and starved? When you see the sheer goodness of God, then the enormity of the sin that said, 'I do not need

you; I'll go my own way', becomes shockingly
apparent.

We cannot all become scholars in Scripture,
but we need to find some wise guide to lead us
to see beyond the simple story that the words
tell. When I first began reading Genesis I found
many questions arose in my mind and I would
go to books to seek clarification, but I would
often be discouraged because I did not understand what they were driving at. Now, quite
simply, I pray and tell God that I do not understand his word and I ask for the Spirit's help.
This does not mean that I get instant illumi-
nations; often several weeks will go by, but
during that time I am taking steps to find
answers. I ask friends, I look in different commentaries, and because my mind is pondering
the question, that means I am on the look-
out and as soon as some insight on the matter
appears, I am quick to notice it. Slowly answers
do emerge. At first it was rather a painstaking
process, but gradually I have acquired knowledge and I have built up a store of information.
It is like doing a jigsaw – initially nothing seems
to connect, then you get little islands of two or
three pieces; these then fit together excitingly
and suddenly the picture emerges.

In the first chapters of Genesis, God is telling
us about the beginnings. Obviously there was
no scribe witnessing the events. God inspired
the author to say what he did say. The scope
of this chapter is not to try and decide who

wrote the account, nor to understand how he or she was inspired. I want to look at the text and dig out its deeper meanings.

We are clearly told that everything God did was good, and yet, deep down, we all have a tendency to blame God when things go wrong. It is interesting how insurance companies refer to 'acts of God' when they are dealing with natural disasters. Genesis is stating clearly that God does not do evil. It is true that it does not explain where evil comes from, but I think we ought to resist the easy way out of blaming God for what goes wrong.

The origin of evil is a question that taxes us all. I knew someone who had a very mischievous daughter. Long before she reached the so-called age of reason, she was into every form of trouble. No one taught her to be naughty; she just seemed to know by instinct what was forbidden. I used to say jokingly that she was proof of original sin; where there was trouble she was in the midst of it. More seriously, we who have passed the age of reason, can detect in ourselves the same trait. Something is wrong with us all. How this should be so, if God made us good in the first place, is something that has bothered mankind since the whole thing began. I do not know where evil comes from, but I know it exists and I can detect it in myself. From the book of Genesis I learn there was a tempter, but where he, or she, came from I do not know. In the book of

Revelation (12:7) we read that there was a battle in heaven. We have no details; we are not told what the battle was about. All we know is that Satan and his followers were cast out of heaven. So even before the creation of the material universe, God had an enemy, and this enemy was bent on spoiling God's new creation. How Satan actually came to do wrong, we do not know, but if God is good, are we right to blame him for the evil we find here on earth?

We should also note that there are two accounts of creation given. This could help us from getting hung up on taking the seven day account literally. In the first account there seems to be a gradation from material things to living plants to animals and finally to the human race, while in the second account people come on the scene fairly early. In the first account we are told that human beings were made in the image and likeness of God, but from the second account we learn that they are unlike God because they are made from the same stuff as the animals. Yet, although they may come from the soil of the earth with the animals, it is clear that they are different from the animals, for God gave the creatures 'all the foliage of plants for food' (1:30) whereas man and woman were given a garden, a park, an attractive place, and it was called 'Delight' (Eden) indicating that they could appreciate beauty. God settled the

27

human beings in this garden and commanded them to cultivate and take care of it.

We are told about the trees in the garden and how Adam is invited to eat of them, and by this we understand that he is invited to explore the richness of the world that he has been asked to master. Two trees in particular are mentioned; one is the tree of life and the other is the tree of knowledge of good and evil. The tree of life stands for God, and the human family are invited to draw their life from him recognising their dependence on him. With regard to the tree of knowledge of good and evil, God expressly forbids Adam from even touching it. It is interesting to notice that Satan questioned Eve about this command and not Adam; Eve had not received the command directly from God and second-hand commands are less forceful than first. What are we to learn from this prohibition? Namely that it is God's prerogative to know good and evil; it is his right to decide what is good and what is evil. In Scripture the word 'know' has the sense of personal experience, and in forbidding man and woman to eat of this tree God is, as it were, saying: 'I do not want you to experience evil. Leave it to me to make decisions with regard to what is good and what is not good for you. Trust in me and obey me.' Here God is treating Adam as *someone*, someone responsible for himself. Human beings are not robots; we are invited to be stewards of God's earth; we will make many decisions as stewards, but we are not lords of the earth and therefore must not make decisions regarding what is good and what is evil. That is the prerogative of God alone. We have been made like God, but we are not God. Love is based on choice. It is not love if it is not chosen. What an extraordinary compliment God pays to the human race in that he makes this creature like unto himself and then invites each individual to say freely: 'I choose you as my God, my source of life.'

In the last chapter I pointed out that we are not just body and soul, but we are body, soul and spirit. This truth made a tremendous difference for me in my understanding of the story of the Fall. For if God communicates with us through our spirit, then anything that can prevent God from doing this will have a devastating effect on us. See how the tempter invites Eve to meet the needs of her body and soul, but not of her spirit. 'The woman saw that the tree was good to eat and pleasing to the eye'; she also saw that 'it was desirable for the knowledge it could give' (3:6). No directing came through her spirit, where God communicates. God, whom Adam and Eve had experienced as utterly trustworthy, is now made to appear by Satan as not totally dependable, and the tragedy is that they trusted the one they did not know, and doubted God whom they had experienced as good. Satan achieved his end – he made Adam and Eve forsake God's way of

29

guidance, and rely for enlightenment on their body and soul. In doing this the human spirit became darkened and we lost the indwelling, guiding Spirit of God. While human beings still remain extraordinarily gifted creatures, we no longer have the inner illumination, and our centre, instead of being God, has shifted to ourselves. We have replaced the light that came from the all-wise God with the light that comes from our own mind, which is incapable of knowing God himself, and can only speculate about him.

How does this affect us?

But what do these remote events say to us who live at such an immense distance from them? If we look honestly into ourselves, I think we will find that we are very much sons and daughters of Adam and Eve. They doubted God's word; have we ever detected the same trait in ourselves? Do we ever find our minds judging God's word? Do not misunderstand me; we must use our minds to comprehend God's word, but when this is hard to do, we can be tempted to judge it or even doubt it. For example, we read in Romans 6 that we are dead to sin. My reaction to that has been to think to myself: 'Not yet; would that I were dead to it.' There my mind is judging Scripture to be wrong and my understanding to be right. It is not a very surprising mistake to make in this instance because, alas, all of us experience that we do commit sins, and if that is so, then how can we be dead to sin? The reason we continue to sin is because we do not stand on the truth that with Christ we have died to the Adam way of life and that there is available to us now the power of the Risen Christ. It is not enough to know this in theory; in some way our belief has to be so real that we can take hold of that truth and actually experience its validity. We carry on sinning because our faith is very weak. We may *know* the truth but it is the acting out of the truth that is so difficult for us. The Holy Spirit can reach your spirit and teach you directly; I can only reach your mind, and that might start a whole deductive process which will only cloud the issue. I will return to this point in a later chapter.

Thus it is very easy for us to doubt God's word. The point I am making is a subtle one; I am not suggesting that we should be gullible, for God made us intelligent creatures, and in the parable of the sower Jesus tells us that when anyone hears the word 'without understanding' then the evil one can snatch it out of his heart (Matt. 13:19). We must allow our minds to be illumined by the word, for this is to live by the Spirit.

Sins of unbelief are not confined to unbelievers. If we want to know what we really believe, we should not ask ourselves 'What do I believe?' because it is all too easy to give lists of things. If we want to know what we believe, we should look and see how we live our life. We might find that the bold words we utter when we profess our faith, are just words when we come down to the nitty-gritty of life. For example, I have found myself, on coming home rather late from a prayer meeting and remembering that I had forgotten to say the Evening Prayer of the Church, wondering if I should then sit down and pray the Evening Prayer. One side of me said, 'You've been praying all evening, surely that was Evening Prayer', while the other part of me was all for fulfilling the letter of the law. That showed what my real attitude was towards God – I could profess with my mouth that he was Father, but in fact my relationship with him was one of anxiety and tension.

In the next chapters we will see how God has restored his indwelling Spirit to our spirit through the death and resurrection of Jesus Christ, but can we honestly say that we live by that Spirit when so many of our decisions are prompted by our body or soul? It is fairly easy to see when it is our body that moves us into action. I am sure you have experienced making resolutions and found that you did not keep them. Maybe you decided that you were eating too many delicacies, say for example cream cakes or rich desserts, and you felt the resolution was firm and serious; but when the cake or dessert was presented, it was just too tempting to resist. There always seems some good reason to say 'just this time'.

Our soul can put us into action in a variety of ways. When I decide to do something because I like it, then my emotions are at work. Or I may decide not to do something because I do not like doing that sort of thing. Fear can prevent us from asking a question; we do not want to appear ignorant, so fear stops us doing the wise thing. When I do something because I want to, then it is my will that is the driving force behind my action. I may want to watch a certain television programme, so I make sure I get into the room first and put the television on before anyone else arrives. The most subtle and often the most deceptive way that the soul directs my actions is through my mind. I now decide to act or not to act according to whether I agree or do not agree. I do something because I hold it to be wise and right, or I refuse to do something because I think it to be wrong; for instance I could go round bathing all the babies in town because it seems like a good idea, but God may not actually want me to do that. Here it is my mind that becomes the final arbitrator and not God's word. All these three faculties – emotions, will and mind – belong to my soul. I think it might be helpful at this point for you to try and recognise the ways in which your soul prompts you to action; each of us is different and for some of us our mind will be the driving force in our lives, while for others our will or our emotions predominate. It is good to be aware of these tendencies and to have some understanding of the way we tick.

Jesus said that we must live by every word that comes out of the mouth of God (Matt. 4:4). It is in our spirit that God reveals his word to us and it is in our spirit that the full content of the word can be grasped. Our minds can appreciate the word but because they are not spirit they cannot take in the spiritual content without the aid of the Holy Spirit. 'What is born of the flesh is flesh; what is born of the Spirit is spirit' (John 3:6). In passing we need to note that the word 'flesh' here does not mean body; it refers to that way of life which does not live by the word of God but lives instead according to its own guidance. I will take this point up again in a later chapter when I will show how respectability can become a subtle substitute for Christianity.

When Adam and Eve chose to live independently of God, they cut themselves off from the guiding light of the Holy Spirit. The children born from Adam and Eve are still gifted children; they have bodies by which they can touch, use and appreciate the world of matter; they have souls that enable them to remember, to think, to decide and to experience emotion; but they lack God's light in their spirits, and since self has replaced God as centre, all these wonderful gifts can be developed and either used for wrong, or for good, noble and upright plans that are man-made and not God inspired. This is a very important point for our minds can conceive good ideas, but good ideas are not necessarily God ideas. St Benedict, in his chapter on humility, quotes from Proverbs, telling us: 'There are ways that seem right to men that can lead to the depths of hell' (Prov. 16:25). Adam's sin was that he wanted autonomy; many of our ideas can be good, worthy and upright but deep down it can be our independent mind that is the driving force and not the word of God.

Before Jesus went back to the Father, he promised that he would send his Holy Spirit, and one of the Spirit's main works would be to convict the world of sin. I hope your heart does not sink when you read that. I do not intend to make you feel terribly guilty, for that is the work of Satan. He it is who accuses the brethren; it is the Holy Spirit who convicts – that is, convinces us that we are sinners – and he only does this in order to comfort us with the truth that there is a remedy in Jesus Christ. It is good to know that Jesus Christ is the saviour, but we can rush to him begging to be saved from all sorts of troubles and fail to ask to be saved from our sin because we are not aware how sinful we are. We did not become sinners the day we committed our first sin. We were born sinners. Again we go back to the account of the Fall in Genesis in order to recognise in ourselves how much we are sons and daughters of our fallen parents. Sin is our attempt to disown God and stand in independence. We resent our God-origin and wish to have autonomy. If we are honest we will see that trait in ourselves. How frustrating our limitations can become. How annoying it can be to have things go wrong. It is amazing how inanimate objects can seem to take on a life of their own when you are trying to organise them.

Is God's will a delight for me, or is it a duty? Intellectually I can know it is good, but emotionally it is often very demanding and not in line with my wants. For example, we all know that it is good to spend some time in prayer; yet how hard it is actually to get down to it. Thousands of reasons crop up to make us postpone the time. I am the most untidy man that has ever lived; I pray in my room and my room is a tip! Whenever I sit down to pray, the thought comes into my mind: 'Why not tidy your room? Now is a good time. The Lord won't mind if you take ten minutes off.' I am sure you will have experienced something similar. How difficult it can be to settle down and pray. All this shows an inner reluctance to be with God. These attitudes lie deep in us, and even though I am a new creation in Chrst, I can still allow these attitudes to take flesh in some external sin. While I can recognise the wrong action I do as sin, often it is easy to fail to see the sin that lies hidden in my attitude.

We were conceived in sin; that does not mean

our parents' act of generation was sinful – it means we are born in sin, we come into existence as hostile to God. God was meant to be the centre of our being, the purpose of our existence. Because of sin he has become off-centre and we have taken the central place in our lives. Therefore God is viewed with suspicion. His very hands stretched out to save us are seen as hands reaching out to unseat us. How is it that God who is so good, that Jesus who was so merciful and compassionate, are not loved naturally by men and women? There is something that distorts our ideas and thoughts of them. This is sin, and there is nothing we can do of ourselves to alter that. All we can do is to admit honestly that that is our condition; then the Spirit will comfort us and show us how 'God loved the world so much that he gave his only Son, so that everyone who believes in him may not be lost but may have eternal life' (John 3:16).

When we begin to see the enormity of sin, when we can admit to God that we often see him as a rival, when we dare to acknowledge that much of our good work comes from selfish motives, then we are in a blessed place to hear that God has a remedy and that it is tailor-made for us.

3

God's Remedy

God dealt with sin by sending his own Son in a body as physical as any sinful body, and in that body God condemned sin. (Rom. 8:3)

We can acquire knowledge either through experience or through learning. Most of those born into Christian families learn about the gospel through being taught. Much depends upon that early presentation. If you had to tell someone the essence of the gospel, I wonder what you would say?

Very early on I learnt about my faith, and I suppose it is not surprising that some truths appeared more attractive than others. The less attractive ones, either because they were mysterious or unpalatable, got pushed into the background. That God had dealt with human sin through the death of Jesus was certainly something I was taught. Unfortunately the language used to convey this doctrine is not helpful. Expressions such as 'atonement', 'making satisfaction for sin', 'bearing God's punishment' are difficult even for mature adults to understand correctly and for young persons they can be horrific. Because I was already pretty suspicious of God, these ideas were offputting. I imagined that Jesus was trying to placate the Father by his terrible death. Theologically, of course, this is nonsense, as it puts Jesus and the Father at opposing ends – Jesus appears to be bargaining with the angry Father by taking on our sufferings. But it is so near the truth that it can be mistaken for the truth. The whole point is that the Father and Son are working together for our rescue. It is through the Father's mercy that he sends his Son; the Son has not come on his own initiative to appease the angry Father.

The way I came to realise the doctrine of the Cross was gradual and painful. After Vatican II we were encouraged to be ecumenical and I am eternally grateful to Protestant pastors who unknowingly made me rethink my understandings. I began looking at my theology and all that I had been taught, and to my utter joy, I started to discover the same teaching as that of my Protestant friends. I have to admit that it needed digging out, and the language often obscured the truth. I feel sure now that if only someone had spelt out to me, in simple language, what the Cross was about, not just dwelling on the immense sufferings of Christ, rousing pity and regret in me, I would have come to an understanding much earlier. Too frequently we assume everyone has a firm grasp of the meaning of the Cross, and so it does not often get preached about. This can have very serious results, because when people do not see the saving power of the Cross of Christ they will look for other solutions to the problems of their lives.

In this chapter I want to explain as clearly as I can what God has done to reconcile us with himself and to give us new life.

God's desire to heal us

We often have the feeling that if we could just get the political scene right then all our troubles would disappear. You have only to listen to any party political broadcast to see how people do believe that right politics will give the answers to our problems. The other false god which promises solutions is the economy. If we could only get that straight then we would live in peace and prosperity.

But the problem is neither politics nor economics – it lies in the heart of humanity. There is a deep flaw within all human beings. We are extremely talented, yet we are very restless. We can aspire to the heights of heaven, yet we can cause utter hell to ourselves and others. We can do the most noble of deeds and yet also the most foul.

God, in making the human race, made people like himself; therefore we can be quite God-like in some of the things we can do. I am

sure we have all experienced those moments
when we seem lifted above ourselves. But the
human being was not made to be God, only
God-like. In trying to snatch to ourselves God-
decisions we threw everything out of balance.
Hence we experience within ourselves this
strange contradiction – nobility and baseness.
This is not solved by politics, nor economics,
nor self-reform programmes; it is solved by God
who so loved the world he had invented and
into which he had put himself, that, when it
went wrong, he sent his Son to take that wrong
into himself and to deal with it as only God
could.

May God forgive me, but I used to wonder
why Jesus, who talked so much about forgiveness, did not just forgive us our sins and start
again. Why all this need for buying back,
making reparation and satisfaction? After all,
when someone messes up the plans I have
made, I can forgive them and say: 'Well, let's
have another go.' Clearly, I did not understand
that sin needs more than forgiveness – it needs
healing. Sin damages the person who commits
it. It leaves them wounded and in need of reparation. A healthy eye delights in the light, but
if I wilfully damage my eye, then the light
becomes painful to it. The light has not
changed, it is my eye that has changed and it
is my eye that needs repairing. When we sin,
we do not damage God, we damage ourselves
and as a result we find God's presence painful.

We not only need forgiving, but we also need repairing so that we can be in relationship with God again.

God's plan to heal human beings of the effects of sin is truly extraordinary. He decides that one of the sons of Adam should be the rescuer of the human race. But how could that possibly happen, since all born of Adam are born in bondage right from the start? God's plan is that his Son, the second Person of the blessed Trinity, should become a man. He does not become man in the way that Adam was made man; there is no second starting of the human race out of nothing; God's Son is born from one of the daughters of Adam. The child born of Mary truly is a son of man, and therefore he can be a legitimate representative of that race. Mary conceives by the overshadowing of the Holy Spirit, so the child born of her is also a Son of God. A son has been born to the human race who has not lost the illumining light of God's Spirit. There now stands among the sons of men One who is not in bondage.

If you have read *Out of the Silent Planet* and *Perelandra* by C. S. Lewis, you will remember how the 'eldil' and all those other beautiful, shadowy creatures that he described so vividly, were astounded at the rumour that Maledil had visited the silent planet in some humble form. So the Father's plan to send his Son as a man must have given the angels of heaven much food for thought. There are those who believe that is why there was a battle in heaven – some angels refused to submit to such a plan. How could the all-holy, all-wise and all-powerful God enter a lower nature and become limited and need to grow in knowledge? I have often wondered how there could ever be a battle in heaven, but it is beyond the scope of this book to explore such thinking. Alas we have become very familiar with the idea that God became man, we need to pause and wonder at the enormity of such a step. Would we be prepared to become a bee to help the world of bees?

As a young man, I always looked on Jesus as being God dressed up as a man, and because he was God he would therefore know everything. That was why he could read people's minds and know what they were thinking, and that was why he did miracles and knew the answer to tricky questions. Then I read F. X. Durwell's *In the Redeeming Christ*, and that started me on a long journey of reassessing my idea of how much of a man Jesus really became. I began asking things like: did Jesus ask a genuine question when the woman touched the hem of his garment and he said: 'Who touched me?' It is difficult to answer that because as God he should know but as man he would not, unless he was a superman or a pseudo-man. Also when he was a boy being taught the skills of carpentry by Joseph, was he standing there with his arms folded saying to himself: 'I actually created the universe' or was he a little boy learning? Today, when people hear about Jesus they discover very early on that he was God and although they are told that he was also a man, the God part overshadows the human part and we find it very difficult to think of him as a man like ourselves. Those who lived with him had no doubt that he was a man; they shared his daily life and they saw him eat, grow tired and need to sleep. They had to make the difficult journey of learning that he was God. I have found tremendous comfort in thinking of Jesus standing where I stand asking questions and having to make decisions. Clearly he 'grew in wisdom' as Scripture tells us, and through the working of the Holy Spirit he came to know who he was and what his mission was. He could not cease to be God but he seems to have renounced the privileges of his position and entered into the nature of humanity so that he could wrestle with Satan, the conqueror of the human race, as a man.

> His state was divine,
> yet he did not cling
> to his equality with God
> but emptied himself
> to assume the condition of a slave,
> and he became as men are,
> and being as all men are,
> he was humbler yet,
> even to accepting death,
> death on a cross. (Phil. 2:6–8)

God's plan is that a man should conquer the one who conquered humans and to make this possible he sent his Son to become a man. By living in human nature and not according to it, Jesus began to overcome the enemy of the human race. Here was a son of Adam who was not living as a son of Adam. He did only the will of the Father. Jesus is doing what the first Adam failed to do; he is living not according to his own ideas, but on 'every word that comes from the mouth of God'. Here is the Christ, the anointed One, who lives by the guiding of the Spirit. He does this in a fallen world and in a fallen nature. He comes to meet the enemy with a nature that is wounded and weak, and with that equipment he takes up the battle.

Since all the children share the same blood and flesh, he too shared equally in it, so that by his death he could take away all the power of the devil, who had power over death, and set free all those who had been held in slavery all their lives by the fear of death. For it was not the angels that he took to himself; he took to himself descent from Abraham. It was essential that he should in this way become completely like his brothers so that he could be a compassionate and trustworthy high priest of God's religion, able to atone for human sins. That is, because he has himself been through temptation he is able to help others who are tempted. (Heb. 2:14–18)

For it is not as if we had a high priest who was incapable of feeling our weaknesses with us; but we have one who has been tempted in every way that we are, though he is without sin. (Heb. 4:15)

The sinless One, having come into a world where there was sin and having adopted a nature wounded by sin, now became accessible to the evil one who relentlessly attacked him since he saw him as a threat to his hold over the sons and daughters of Adam. It is not surprising that Jesus, after hearing the confirming words at his baptism 'You are my beloved Son in whom I am well pleased', should have been tempted in the desert with the very words: '*If* you are the Son of God, tell these stones to turn into loaves.' One of our race conquers Satan, the prince of this world, by living as a man in this world, yet never submitting to the dictates of him who ruled all people.

Another way that Jesus conquers Satan is by unseating him from his position as prince of this world. When Adam and Eve, who were made to be masters here on earth, submitted to Satan's deception, Satan became the ruler. In his public life Jesus attacks Satan in all the places where he has taken up his abode as lord. For this work he needed the anointing of the Holy Spirit so that he could confront the evil one. When Jesus was accused of casting out evil spirits by the power of Beelzebul, the prince of devils, he retorted that it was through the power of the Holy Spirit that he did such things: 'If it is through the Spirit of God that I cast devils out, then know that the kingdom of God has overtaken you' (Matt. 12:28).

The kingdom of God is not a geographical place – it is anywhere where God's rule is carried out. Jesus has come to restore God's rule on earth; so every time he meets the evil one pretending to be in charge, Jesus shows who is the master by commanding Satan to depart. I think that rather curious verse about binding the strong man first before you can plunder his house, refers to the fact that Jesus has come to bind Satan so that he can win back what rightfully belongs to the Father: 'How can anyone make his way into a strong man's house and burgle his property unless he has tied up the strong man first? Only then can he burgle his house' (Matt. 12:29). Every time Jesus meets the strong one exercising his unlawful authority he drives him out. The gospel stories are full of people being delivered from the power of the devil.

In his public life Jesus healed the sick, thus showing that he did not see sickness as part of the kingdom of God. I have heard people mistakenly saying to the sick: 'Well, it is God's will.' True, it is his permissive will, but not his direct will. If it is God's express will, then why did Jesus heal the sick, and how can we justify our going to hospitals and doctors, if God should want us sick? Clearly, it is not God's direct will that we should be sick. God can, of course, use sickness and draw good from it; but that does not make sickness a good thing in itself. Quite simply, sickness is an evil. This does not mean that a sick person is evil; it means that they are being afflicted by evil. Jesus came to re-establish God's rule here on earth and so whenever he meets evil in any form he comes against it showing who the rightful Master is. The kingdom of God is not yet here amongst us in all its glory but because it has already begun here on earth, we see it now and then breaking through into the present. Healings do still happen today.

To be prince of this world is a very high title so we should not be surprised if this prince should be able to use things of this world for his purpose. If I say that the storm which broke onto the boat the Lord was sleeping in was demon caused, I do not then mean that all bad weather is demon instigated. The evil one can use things of this earth for his reasons; the Lord overrules his commands showing that he is the Lord of the earth.

So Jesus overcame the evil one by living in flesh yet never submitting to the one who had conquered flesh. He also overcame by ousting the usurper from the places where he had taken up his abode. But all these victories only affect the person Jesus; he is living a human life free of sin but this does not free the race from sin.

When Jesus heals a sick person, it is Jesus who conquers the sickness; the sick person remains vulnerable to further attacks. We must now look at the main reason for Jesus becoming a man. This is the whole purpose of his coming among us and dying and rising to a new life.

Jesus' death and resurrection

I always found it very difficult to understand why Jesus had to die. Somehow it made me fear the Father who, in some way, was placated and satisfied by this terrible death. I could not see how death could blot out sin; I could not see why Jesus had to die for my sin, and, if his death took away my sins, how was it that I still sinned? All these thoughts troubled me and made me uneasy about this part of Christianity. I could feel attracted to the God of nature, I could find interest in books on prayer, I wanted to live a spiritual life. I was drawn to the goodness of the Lord – but all talk about sacrifice and atonement was very strange and mystifying. I have given an immense amount of time and effort in searching into this mystery and only gradually, and very gradually, has it begun to yield light. Here in the sunset of my life I think I have begun to grasp its meaning. I hope I can share some of this with you using the simplest ideas I can find. It would be very appropriate if you paused at this moment and asked the Holy Spirit to lead you into an understanding of his truth.

If it was winter, and we were standing around a huge bonfire in the Arctic Circle, then, if anyone should turn away from the fire and walk off, they would go into the dark and the cold. It would not be the bonfire putting them in the dark and cold, it would be the consequence of their choice to turn and walk away from the source of light and heat. When we sin, we choose something other than God. We turn away from the One who is the source of life and goodness. To turn away from that which gives life, is to turn towards that which will not give life. The non-life that follows is a consequence of our choice. It is not God punishing us with death; rather he is saying: 'If you leave me, the source of life, then there is no alternative. Even I cannot prevent the result from happening. I, and I alone, am the One who gives life.' When I began to look at God's punishment for sin as a consequence of sin, I started to see the word 'punishment' in a new way. I realised that it was right and just that such serious consequences should follow turning one's back on God. Of course I am talking here about responsible sin. Adam and Eve's sin was very responsible and deliberate. They chose not to live by God, but by their own decisions. The result was that they lost their ability to know God in their spirit; they could now only speculate about him in their minds. Here was a major disaster; God's special creature was now unable to know him and to die in that state would mean eternal separation from him.

Darkness and light cannot be together. If you have a dark room and you bring light into it, the darkness has to go. Notice that you cannot bring darkness into a lighted room, you can only remove the light and the darkness will return. This just shows that light is stronger than darkness. Let us apply the same principle to a deeper truth. Evil and God cannot be in relationship. God made the human being good. God wanted to have relationship with men and women so he created them in his own image and likeness. But the human race did evil and made it impossible to remain in relationship with God. However, God loves people, so he comes up with a remedy. He sends his Son to become a man, and we have seen above that he really became a man. There is no sin in him for it was through the Holy Spirit that he took flesh. Here is the man that God intended Adam to be. The incredible plan of the Father is that this beloved Son of his should take on himself the sins of humanity. The Son willingly consents to this. Jesus did not sin but he allowed in some way all the sins of the human race to be loaded onto him and he experienced the consequences of sin – separation from the source of life, namely death. Scripture goes very far in describing this for it says: 'God made the sinless one into sin' (2 Cor. 5:21).

Just imagine what a cost that was for Jesus. He, who spent himself in doing the Father's will, now felt himself removed from the Father. He would have experienced the justice of God being worked out on him for the very nature of God makes it impossible for sin and God to be in relationship. The physical agony of crucifixion is terrible, but for Jesus to experience the separation from the Father caused by our sins, is something we can hardly begin to fathom. The cry 'Why have you forsaken me?' took on for me an awful meaning when I began to see Jesus was bearing the justice of God in my place. What must the cost have been to the Father to see his righteous judgement carried out on his Son? God the Father spared Abraham that sacrifice but he willingly gave us his own Son.

But why was all this necessary? Here we must try to understand God's extraordinary plan. Because Jesus was God, every action of his would have infinite value. Therefore when he took on himself the consequences of our sins, he would have met those consequences to the full. The result of sin was that the human race was incapable of having relationship with God and was unable to know God's will, and thus unable to fulfil it. That barrier was now removed, because Jesus' death had such infinite value that death, real death, was no longer due to those who belonged to Christ. So, by entering into death, Jesus paid the full debt for sin. He did not pretend to die, he actually died; he bore the debt completely.

Thus the death of Jesus has been the means by which our sins are forgiven. Earlier we saw that the healing of sin requires more than forgiveness – for, after all, forgiveness does not save us from sinning again; we need in some way to be set free from sinning. In dying Jesus met the demands of sin, but when he entered into death, an innocent man entered into the region where only sinners go. The kingdom of death has no right or power to keep captive anyone who had never sinned. When Jesus paid the full debt for sin by dying, death could not keep hold of him so he broke out of the bonds of death and returned to his body, causing it to rise to new life. The resurrection does not mean that Jesus came back to life in the same way that Lazarus did; no, he rose to a new life. Here was a son of Adam, now totally and utterly freed from the bondages of Adam. Here was the conqueror of Satan, who could never be personally attacked again, save through the members of his body still living on earth. Here was the new Adam and from him a new race would spring. Those born from the old Adam can have a new birth through water and the Holy Spirit into this new Adam. This new race would still dwell on earth in the fallen world, but by their daily choosing to live in the new life that they have received, they could escape from the old Adam way. The new life that they are called to live is not in the realm of feeling, nor in the realm of experience in the sense of experience leading to faith; rather it is in the realm of faith which will lead to experience. It is interesting to see how often Jesus said to those who were healed by him, 'It is your faith that has set you free'.

When I began to see all this with my inner eye, then familiar gospel texts took on a new meaning. Words such as 'I am the Way, the Truth and the Life' suddenly made immense sense. I understood now that there was no way to heaven save through being united to Jesus Christ. I saw Christianity as a process of being 'Christed', of being transformed into the One who had a right to go to the Father. What a terrible tragedy it is when Christianity is seen as rules and regulations whereby we merit our way into heaven. Jesus has told us, 'There is no way to the Father save through me'. This does not make it all easy; our self-will rebels against depending on another. If someone offers us a gift, it does not become ours until we accept it, take hold of it, unwrap it and use it. Christ has done something immense for us, and he is forever holding out to us this gift of new life in him. The spiritual path is the art of living that new life.

4

Gifts Have to be Received

Unless a wheat grain falls on the ground and dies, it remains only a single grain; but if it dies, it yields a rich harvest. (John 12:24)

I wonder if you have ever prepared a gift, gone to quite a lot of trouble over it, and had it hardly noticed when you gave it? I remember once making someone a Christmas card. I took a great deal of care, wrote a special text on it, and sent it off with excitement and some expectation. I got a card back, which I suppose was an acknowledgement because I do not think this person would ordinarily have sent me one, but absolutely no reference was made to my own card. The disappointment was really quite deep. If we feel hurt when others fail to appreciate what we do for them, imagine how much more we must hurt God when we refuse to accept the gift he is offering us in his Son.

Gifts need both to be given *and* received before they can properly be called our own. Unless we unwrap and use what we have been given, we do not profit by the gift. If I am thirsty and am given a cool drink, I am not refreshed until I drink what I have been given. So also, it is not enough to know what God has done for me through his Son; I need to appropriate his gift, and this is a lifetime's job. If a lemon branch is grafted onto an orange tree, and the graft takes, then we have a very interesting situation – we have a lemon branch with orange life entering into it. Not being a botanist I do not know what fruit will be produced, but the point of the illustration is that the lemon branch is now living with a new kind of life, and that new life has to be continually accepted if the fruit is going to be produced; if ever it rejected that new life, then the branch would die.

In the last chapter we looked at what Jesus Christ was doing for us by dying and rising from the dead. We tried to see what he did. In this chapter we want to look at how his dying and rising affect us.

Before Jesus went back to his Father, he promised that after he had gone the Holy Spirit would be sent: 'I shall ask the Father, and he will give you another Advocate to be with you for ever' (John 14:16).

In the first Letter of St John, Jesus is referred to as our advocate with the Father (2:1–2). An advocate is someone who pleads the cause of another in the court of law. It is comforting to know that Jesus is at the right hand of the Father making intercession for us. So, when

Jesus tells us that we will have 'another Advocate', does that mean we will now have two intercessors in heaven? In the text quoted above we are told that this new Advocate will 'be with us for ever', and in John 14:26 we learn that he will teach us everything and remind us of all that Jesus has said. He has come to plead the cause of Jesus with us. This is the main reason for God sending the Holy Spirit. He comes so that he may work on all, prompting, guiding, leading and causing everyone to question and search for the reasons of life. The Holy Spirit is not confined to believers; he is forever prompting, nudging, using every situation for his purposes. Not all of us have been able to meet Jesus in the flesh; the Spirit of God has been sent to challenge everyone born into this world, confronting them with the One who has risen from the dead. He deals with us as individuals, never forcing but also never desisting.

In the last chapter we saw how Jesus' death dealt with our actual sins, and how his resurrection enables us to live a new life, whereby we need not sin. For years I found it very difficult to see how Jesus' death could cancel my sins and remove the barrier between me and God. My understanding was blocked because the doctrine of atonement seemed to portray an angry God who could only be placated by a blood sacrifice. These wrong ideas of God seemed to be confirmed for me by the fact that the Old Testament was full of blood sacrifices.

This ignorance virtually meant that I did not take hold of what Jesus had done by his death and resurrection since I could not accept a God, who was meant to be good, acting in what appeared to be such a cruel way. In other words false ideas about God were successfully preventing me from putting my faith and trust in those very things he had done to save me. I do not think that I consciously rejected the doctrine of atonement, but rather I consigned it to the realm of mystery, and I vaguely hoped my understanding of it was wrong.

This leads me to see how important it is to try to understand the gospel and not just to believe it. Certainly it is more important to believe than to understand, but we can often be prevented from having a healthy belief because of some misunderstanding. Faith is beyond reason, not contrary to it. Thank God that today the Church is refinding her mission to teach and explain. All over the country small study groups are springing up.

This, alas, can produce a different kind of problem. People can mistake understanding for believing. That brings me back to my illustration about the accepting of gifts. It is not enough to know that Jesus has borne my sins; I must act on that truth. Fear and anxiety about our sins can plague us, and Satan will certainly cash in on such tendencies by trying to convince us that we will not receive forgiveness. This is where strong, determined action is required.

God's revelation to us is that his Son has borne our sins, and it is on that truth that we must direct our lives. When Jesus took our sins and died for them, this act of his had infinite value because he is God, and so all that blocks a sinner from God has now been removed. My sins, your sins, and even all the sins yet to be committed, have been dealt with. This does not mean that universal pardon has been applied to all; it means that there is pardon for all who will go to collect it. This involves admitting my sin; for I cannot receive pardon for something that I do not admit to. When we confess our sins, Jesus says to his Father: 'Father, I have dealt with that.' It is then the Spirit's work to apply the saving death and rising of Jesus to the sinner. That is why the Holy Spirit is known as the sanctifier – he is constantly applying the healing, saving work of Jesus to those who humbly ask for it. Needless to say, this does not give us the liberty to sin and then claim the forgiveness won by Christ, because genuine confession of sin requires regret and repentance.

Standing on the truth that Christ has borne our sins does not mean that we try to feel this truth. We are not asked to work up our emotions or feelings; we are simply asked to accept the truth of God's word. This requires discipline; it means denying our anxieties, our arguments, our fears. We have to stand deliberately on what God has said. This is what it means to live by the Spirit. We take the words that God has spoken and we trust in their promise and refuse to be blown about by every wind.

New life

Sin needs more than forgiveness; it needs taking away. We are weak, and although we may regret our actions and ask forgiveness, this does not stop us from committing that sin again. Now we must try to understand how the resurrection of Christ is our hope of living a new life.

Jesus took to himself the nature of Adam, but he never lived according to its demands. In his obedience to his Father, he was overcoming the one who had overcome the human race. Here was one of the sons of Adam conquering the conqueror of the sons of Adam. Jesus spent his life dying to the human nature he had taken to himself. On Calvary, he died in fact to that nature. He laid it down. When the Father raised him to life, he did not bring him back to the life he had laid down; he raised him to a new life, a life inaccessible to evil, a life that was powerful, a life that made him Lord with a right to reign on earth and in heaven. Manifestly the Jesus who kept appearing to his disciples after he had risen was very different from the Jesus they had walked the roads with in

Galilee. Yet the person was the same; he was still man, but he was transcendent, risen, new.

The plan of the Father is to have this new life transmitted to the children of Adam. Life comes through birth, so how can these children of Adam receive this life since they have already been born? They must be born again, Jesus said. This new birth is accomplished through water and the Holy Spirit. God's plan is not to reform the Adam life; his plan is to do away with it. It must die and be replaced by this new life of the risen Christ. St Paul teaches us that when we were baptised, we were baptised into the death of Christ, so that we could imitate him in his resurrection. This was clearly demonstrated in the old rite of baptism – the going under the water signified the dying and burial, the coming up the rising to new life in Christ.

How important it is to understand that new life is *new life*. It is not our old life enhanced, improved, renovated. It is something new. It is the act of believing what God has done for us through the death and resurrection of his Son that makes the work of Jesus effective in us. Any ignorance as to what has been done, can render God's saving power inoperative in us. Any thinking that the new life we have received is only old life improved can successfully block the power of the Cross from having its effect in our lives. Again how important it is for us to know and understand what God has done for

61

us so that we can put our faith in his action. Ignorance is the best way of rendering the gospel impotent, for it is faith that activates the power of God, and when there is ignorance as to what God has done, then acts of faith cannot be made.

I meet people today whose understanding of the Christian faith is something as follows:

> Jesus came to teach us what to do. He told us to love God, to love our neighbour, even love our enemy. He told us not to lie, cheat or be unfair. To sum up, he told us to be good. His teachings were not popular, so they did away with him by nailing him to a cross. To prove to all that he was God, he rose from the dead. This makes his teachings very important and our lives will be judged on how well we have put his teachings into practice. Hopefully after we die we will hear: 'Well done, good and faithful servant, enter into the kingdom prepared for you and the angels'.

There is much truth in this and that is what makes it all the more deceptive. The death of Jesus is just seen as a regrettable event, which really need not have happened; so the faith called for by such teaching stretches only to the fact that Jesus was God and therefore his teaching must be sound. There is no call for faith in what Jesus did by dying and rising again, and that cuts at the very root of the gospel. When faith is not centred on the main act of the gospel, the death and resurrection of the Lord, then the power of the Cross is blocked. People who believe this version of the gospel may be very nice, respectable, law-abiding citizens, but is it new life that they are living or old life improved?

We must not imagine that we can do nothing with our natural life. We can learn to mask our real self. We can smile when we would rather not; we can look calm when in fact we are agitated; appear welcoming when we are bored. Respectability can mask itself as Christianity. A nice church, nice people, a nice service – all very decent, proper and right.

As a novice, I was expected to spend some time each day in personal prayer. This took place at a certain time and one was expected to be there. But your presence did not mean you actually prayed. You may have looked prayerful, recollected, even holy, but that could have all been external. This raises a very serious question: how do we learn to live by this new life that is in us? Do we just sit around hoping that one day it will take over? This question has bothered me for a long time and I have given years of thought to it. It first presented itself to me in this form: 'If I have new life in me and I am a new creation, how is it that I still sin?' At first I began to think along the lines, 'I am not yet a new creation; hopefully one day I will be', but that is to deny Scripture which clearly says: For anyone who is in Christ, there is a new creation; the old creation has gone, and now the new one is here' (2 Cor. 5:17).

Shoddy thinking, imagining that new life is only old life dusted up, successfully stops us making an act of faith in the truth that Jesus has won us new life. We must stand on what God has told us and not on what we either feel or experience. I am beginning to understand that new life cannot be lived by muscle, but that it grows in us as we call on its power to be in our lives. I believe it is very deliberate acts of trust that the power of the Cross is greater than the power of sin in me which make this life grow. Our faith needs exercising. Once we are in Christ, we have a new life, and that life has to grow and develop. A healthy new-born baby has a full human body. There is nothing more to be added – all is there; but it needs development and growth; it has to learn how to use all its various parts. So, too, with this new life in Christ; it is all there, but it needs to grow and develop, and we have to learn how to use it. Once we begin to think it is not there, but is something yet to come to us, then we are not accepting in faith what Jesus has done, because we do not believe he has done it. If I deny that I already have new life, then I virtually paralyse that new life.

What makes it so difficult to live this new life is that there is no new set of muscles to use. I wonder what you do when you see someone approaching whom you do not like? (Note that God does not command us to like everyone; he commands us to love them, and that is quite different.) We can begin by calling on our natural powers to be nice. We can even smile and say the right things. We may even deceive the person and then they stay longer than we expected and sooner or later they will touch a soft spot and we blow our stack. Then we go away from that encounter angry with the person, angry with ourselves and making resolutions that next time we will succeed. But surely we are right to assume that some effort must be made on our part, especially if we have never yet experienced the new life taking over. I do not believe that it is wrong to put on a smile and to do our best, provided we know that this is not the real thing. However our first action must be to declare that the power of the Cross is greater than the power of unlove in us. Having called on God, we then offer him our poor effort. As our trust in the power of the Cross grows through the Holy Spirit's teaching and through our praise and thanks to God, we will begin to experience its reality in our lives. Larry Christenson, an American Lutheran pastor, gave this illustration: he said that if you want to build a concrete archway, you first make a wooden form for the arch. It is not the arch itself, only a form into which the concrete must be poured. Once the concrete has set, the wooden form is taken away. Our small acts of charity are only the wooden form – they are not the real thing. We offer them to God and ask him to pour into our efforts the real thing. In time he will.

Our task is not to overcome, but to allow Jesus to overcome in us. We are not called to fight with our own power, but to fight with the power of the risen Christ. In the Letter to the Ephesians (6:10) we are told 'to grow strong' not with our own power but 'with the strength of his power'. This does not mean that there is no effort on our part; our effort is to use Christ. If you row a boat, then the boat moves by your power. When you sail a boat it is moved by the power of the wind, but you have to cooperate with the wind. Holiness is not something that we achieve; it is something that God achieves in us if we will let him. All our efforts are to allow the work of Jesus to become effective in us.

Another reason why it is so difficult to live by this new life is quite simply the fact that we do not want to live by it. Deep down in all of us is the originating sin, the sin that says, 'I'll do it on my own. I'll manage; I do not need help'. It is the sin of Adam when he said: 'I'll go my own way. I'll think it out. I am intelligent.' We were created to be God-centred; sin has made us self-centred. We find it very hard to accept salvation as a gift; we would like to be able to take some credit. Naaman resisted

doing what the prophet Elisha told him to do.
He had hoped that he would be asked to perform a noble, heroic deed, so that he could
claim some credit for his healing (2 Kings 5).
This drive is deep within us all; even our desire
to serve God and do what is right can spring
from our ambition to be thought good. We can
do what is expected of us for wrong reasons.
Man-made goodness has something unattrac-
tive about it. It is hard to describe, but deep
down we recognise it – it is just too good, too
right. Genuine holiness is awe-inspiring and
makes us want to give God the praise for what
he can do in our sin-prone nature.

Scripture refers to our death in Christ both
as something already achieved and as something yet to be accomplished. We read:

> All those who belong to Christ Jesus have
> crucified self with all its passions and desires.
> (Gal. 5:24 *New Jerusalem Bible*)

> We must realise that our former selves have
> been crucified with him to destroy this sinful
> body and to free us from the slavery of sin.
> (Rom. 6:6)

All that is very definite and final, yet we also
read:

> That is why you must kill everything in you
> that belongs only to earthly life: fornication,
> impurity, guilty passion, evil desires . . .
> (Col. 3:5)

But if by the Spirit you put an end to the misdeeds of the body you will live. (Rom. 8:13)

We must remember that we can live our lives on many levels. We can be controlled by our bodies, our souls or by what the Spirit of God reveals to us. Whatever choice we make it is not a once-and-for-all decision. If we choose to live by the Spirit, constantly we have to continue to make that choice. Just as when someone decides to sing a song, they have to continue in that choice until the end of the song. It is not a matter of feeling. Daily we have to choose to live the new life we have received. Daily we need to believe that the power of the Cross is greater than any other power we may encounter. We will not feel this truth; we may not even experience it, but experiences must not direct our lives. This does not mean that experiences are not important. The Church I grew up in was very suspicious of them, and I think I now understand the reason why. To believe something because I experience it, is not very sound. Very often I experience God as absent, far-away, remote and if I allow these feelings to influence me, I will feel low and abandoned. Sometimes, though not often, I feel God is present, but that does not make him present; he is always present because he has said so. Thus to base my life on my experiences would be very unwise. But if I trust in God's promises, I will experience his fidelity – that sort of experience is good and right and should be expected.

The kingdom of God is not here in all its fullness. We are in an unique period in history, where the enemy has been defeated but is not yet chained up. Scripture tells us that he roars around like a lion, but we must resist him, strong in faith (1 Peter 5:8–9). We have received the first-fruits of the Spirit in our own spirit: 'The Spirit himself and our spirit bear united witness that we are children of God' (Rom. 8:16). But our own bodies are not yet redeemed: ' . . . we too groan inwardly as we wait for our bodies to be set free' (Rom. 8:23).

So already we are a new creation, yet we have to continue to make the choice to live as such. Only experience can teach us that if we live on the level of the Spirit and are directed by him, then we will be set free. Reason finds it very difficult to grasp this, and the western world is largely mind-controlled.

God has told us that we can have, or do have, new life in Christ. The more we exercise our belief in this fact and endeavour to live by its message, the more we will experience the power of the risen Lord in us. As this new life grows in us, so our actions will begin to be new as well. The battle lies in the decision who is going to control our minds?

5

The God Who Speaks

Where were you when I laid the earth's
   foundations?
Tell me, since you are so well-informed!
Who decided the dimensions of it, do you
   know?
Or who stretched the measuring line across
   it?
What supports its pillars at their bases?
Who laid its cornerstone
when all the stars of the morning were singing
   with joy,
and the Sons of God in chorus were chanting
   praise? (Job 38:4–7)

There is a battle going on for our mind.
Whoever, or whatever, controls that, controls
us. Our bodily desires can control us, or our
own thinking can be our master, or we can
allow the Holy Spirit to direct and guide us.
The choice is ours. But we were born with a
nature biased towards self rather than God, and
we find a battle raging within us. St Augustine
wrote that 'Our hearts are restless until they

70

rest in Thee' – alas, we imagine that restlessness
can be assuaged by self-gratification, and this is
the deception at the very root of our being;
what cannot be totally satisfying appears to be
so, and what God offers, which is our only way
of hope, seems to our jaundiced eyes to be
stony, threatening and unprofitable.

The question I want to wrestle with in this
chapter is how do we allow the Holy Spirit to
control our thinking? The obvious answer is to
read Scripture where God reveals himself and
his plans to us. While I agree that the word of
God is of utmost importance, I have to question
if it is not too simplistic to expect that anyone
will discover God just by reading his word.
Long before we open the Bible or have it
opened to us, we have already formed a picture
of God. This picture can come through a chance
remark, through a feeling of awe or fear felt in
a strange place, or through saying some prayer
for a desperate need that, apparently, was not
answered.

I know someone who had a deep-rooted fear
of God. It was not hard to trace from where
that fear came – a domineering father had so
destroyed the idea 'father' that when God was
described in this way a terrible picture was
conceived. As I say it was fairly easy to see
where the problem came from, but it was no
simple job to erase that first impression. This
man was not well versed in Scripture and I
wanted him to meet the merciful Lord who

forgave sinners and healed the sick. But my advice to read Scripture was disastrous for it only confirmed his fear of God. Every passage where Jesus was speaking to the Pharisees and correcting them, my friend took to himself; every act of mercy carried out by the Lord, he saw as being done to those who in some sense were worthy. This image that my friend had of God overrode everything that Scripture was trying to say. He was not able to hear the truth and even when I pointed out how illogical he was – for it says clearly that Jesus came for sinners – he just could not believe that this applied to him. This shows how important early ideas of God are and how easy it is to pick up false impressions.

I wonder if you have had the experience of seeing a film of a novel you once read? Often I have been disappointed by the way a favourite character was portrayed. On going back to the book and checking carefully how the author described this person, I have discovered that I had taken liberties and had imagined the person as I wanted them to be and not as the author was describing them. None of us has seen God and therefore we are tempted to form our own idea of him and this idea can be quite contrary to what God has said about himself. Once we have formed our picture, it will leap in and colour our thinking every time we hear the word 'God'.

I feel that it is very important for these

pictures of God to be exposed to the light. We can be frightened even to admit to ourselves what we really feel about God. We have been told that he is perfect, all-good and all-merciful, and we can so easily trot out these answers when we are questioned about him. But we need to be desperately honest here and ask, 'Is God good in my eyes? Is he someone I can trust absolutely, or is he someone I know I ought to trust?' Too often the God we harbour in the depths of our being bears little or no resemblance to the picture Jesus drew of the Father when he told us the parable of the prodigal son.

My early impressions of God, picked up somewhere in childhood, had so coloured my ideas of God, that no matter what was said about him, these deep-rooted notions rendered every new picture invalid, ineffective and unconvincing. It was not a conscious process, it was a pattern of thinking that I had fallen into. I never dared to share those pictures I had of God with anyone; I feared they would be thought blasphemous. I now see how important it is to bring these shadowy thoughts out into the full light of day. When they remain in the unconscious, they are indistinct, obscure, fuzzy and unclear. St Paul urged: '. . . every thought is our prisoner, captured to be brought into obedience to Christ' (2 Cor. 10:4–5).

To be wrong about God is to be wrong about everything. Hence there is a serious battle to control our minds. So how do we begin to get a true picture of God? That is not an easy question to answer. I think we can be helped by looking at how we get to know people. It is not enough just to hear them speak, we need to watch them, see how they behave, how they handle things, are they true to their word? Are they moody, gentle, thoughtful? Slowly we begin to piece together a picture. So it must be with God. We need to tune into all the ways he speaks with us. I needed to reconcile the God of the fields with the God I met in church. I am sure that if I had understood that the God who spoke to me in church was the same as the One I met in the woods, I would have listened with a different attitude.

How important it is to find a wise guide to walk with us as we set out on this pilgrimage. Alas, parents, who should have been our first guides, often fought shy of the job, and those early impressionable years were lost. This has meant that schools have often had to build on foundations that were not there. How good it would have been if someone had confirmed for me that what I contacted in sunshine, colour, or in the bold sweep of hills, was a glimmer of him who dances in the skies. What a tragedy it was that the God of church was so forbidding. Before he ever opened his mouth, I felt condemned; hence I dreaded to hear what he had to say.

As we look at the various ways God speaks

to us we must remember that no idea I have of God *is* God, and no idea that you have of God *is* God. Therefore our ideas of him are in constant need of change. We are tempted to wrap him up in definitions, tie him down to our human concepts, box him up in our doctrines. How right it is that God should forever burst out of these confines, shatter our images and make us realise he is greater than our wildest thoughts.

When we get to know people we learn about them through all sorts of different channels. We can discover a lot just by seeing how they behave, the way they touch things, how they walk; all these things can convey to us certain insights. So, too, it is with God; simply looking at the things he has made can tell me much about him. What manner of being must he be who can create colour, sunshine, water? Take water; it is such ordinary stuff, yet really it is such extraordinary stuff. It has no colour, no odour, no shape, but it is terribly real. You can ski right across the top of it. It washes, refreshes, gives life, takes it away. What must he be like who invented it, and so much of it? How important it is to take time to look and see and wonder. Try to imagine the world as a black and white photograph – then, hopefully, you will become aware of colour. What must he be like who could think up red, blue, yellow?

We need to take time to listen to the breathing of the world around us. Those of us who live in vast cities have cut ourselves off from the wonder of nightfall, the rising of the sun, the subtle change in seasons. All of us, wherever we are, are often so absorbed in our own worlds that we fail to notice the beauty of nature. As I mentioned earlier, I used to live and teach in the USA, and there the colours of the leaves in autumn are much more rich and remarkable than in Britain. One day, as I was walking towards the gym with a young student, I noticed the marvellous greens, yellows and reds of the leaves on the trees, and I said to the student, 'Look at that! Isn't it wonderful!' He became interested but could not discover what I was looking at and begged me to tell him. I teased him for a while and then finally told him I was referring to the leaves. 'Oh,' he said with obvious disappointment, 'is that all?'

Even our learning can take the mystery out of life – rain is no longer God providing the earth with its needed refreshment, it is just moisture gathered off the sea, now cooling and falling as rain. We do a sort of violence to the seasons by producing daffodils in autumn, chrysanthemums in spring and strawberries at Christmas. This, of course, is not wrong and I find it difficult to say why it makes me uneasy. But there are some so-called advances in knowledge which are actually harmful and which prove us to be poor stewards of our world. Insecticides that poison birds and remove some species, thus producing an imbalance in nature, seem to me to show a very uncaring attitude towards God's wonderful creation. In our greed for profit we over-fish the seas, we over-produce crops; we export western techniques to poorer countries and destroy ancient cultures and valued ways of living, all in the name of prosperity. We are not lords of the earth in the sense that we can do with it what we wish. We are co-workers with the One who made it all and invited us to share in its development.

So, God speaks to us through the world around us. All the beauty that I see in creation must in some way be in him who made it. We should strive to think of him in new ways, we should try to break out of our stereotyped manner of speaking with him. Perhaps we should address him as 'the One who makes the rainbows', or as 'the One who listens to the hills', and thus begin to form a new picture, a picture of awe and beauty to replace our dull and faded images.

God also speaks to us through the world within us. If I can get excited over a tree in full flower, how much more ought I to get excited over the God who invented you and me! Alas, not many of us were taught to love ourselves in the correct way. I have found it helpful to think of God forever continuing to create me. A song exists only as long as the singer continues to sing it. We only exist because God chooses to continue singing us into being. How important it is to appreciate the fact that we are alive solely because someone wishes it that way. What a gift it is to see, to hear, to be able to come and go, to touch things, to feel the rough and the smooth. I remember once trying to experience what it was like to be blind. I put my hands over my eyes, but I could still see light seeping through my fingers. One day I actually got into a room where no chink of light penetrated, but in some way I saw, I saw dark. Later on someone told me that to experience what it is to be blind all you have to do is to look in your left shoe with your left foot. You do not see black, you just do not see!

We need to have a healthy appreciation of ourselves and our gifts. Clearly, self-boasting and arrogance are wrong, but it is equally wrong to despise oneself and to consider oneself an unfortunate mistake. Much harm was done in the past in the name of humility, and we need to find a right balance. Who has ever plumbed the mystery of their own being? Or who has understood the subtle moods that come and go like clouds in a summer sky? Who has not asked the question, 'Just who am I?', and not sensed a certain unseating of oneself as an answer is sought? Hopefully all these searchings bring us face to face with the One who tells us from all eternity that he has chosen us to be.

Also what a privilege it is to be allowed to see into the wonder of another person. I remember when a young boy called Mark shared something of himself. He told me that he liked to catch frogs. I thought this a rather interesting thing for a child to want to do and so I asked him all about it. He began to tell me about the tremendous excitement and sense of adventure he felt as he set out to look for frogs, and about the lovely smell of the marshes as he approached the pond. And I asked him: 'Surely when you get to the pond the frogs aren't sitting there waiting for you? How do you catch them?' He said: 'Oh no, of course they've all gone back into the pool as soon as they've heard me coming.'

'Well, what do you do about it?'

'I get right to the edge of the pond and then I stand there, and I pretend I'm a tree.'

'Well yes, that's lovely, but what happens?'

'Well, I may have to stay a very long time, but if I keep very still it may be that the surface of the pond breaks and two eyes will look out. And if I'm lucky, but it doesn't often happen, they may come out and they may sit on the smooth stones within my reach.'

Of course, now I'm caught up in the story and I want to know what's going to happen, so I ask him to tell me more. 'If they do come within my reach, then of course I have to make my move and suddenly I will make a lunge.'

'And do you ever catch them?'

'Oh very rarely.'

'And what happens if you do?'

'Ah well, that's the whole triumph. I've caught my frog!'

'And what do you do with him?'

'Oh, I tickle him under the chin and I like to feel his slimy skin, and I envy him because he doesn't go to school.'

'And then what?'

'I let him go.'

You can imagine the frog sinking back into the green pool thinking, 'What was all that about?' But it's not the frog I'm interested in; it's the little boy. By telling me what he liked to do, he told me a great deal about himself: a very gentle boy, very patient, very outgoing. And so whenever I hear the word 'Mark' now I immediately think of the boy who liked to catch frogs. Somehow I've come in contact with him.

Sadly we are often afraid to let others get to know us at a deep level; we fence around talking about the weather, good places for holidays, the cost of living, when it would be much more revealing, but also much more terrifying, if we asked each other when we last wept and why; or if we shared what we think about as we walk around. That would be very revealing. We need to say to someone, 'Tell me who you are. What do you think and dream about? Tell me about the real you.' We should be grateful when such opportunities do arise for they are moments of grace and they draw us closer to one another. They also draw us closer to God, for what manner of being must he be who made so many of us, each different, each unique?

So, we begin to meet God in a variety of ways and we start to weave our understanding of him through many, many impressions. But if I am to avoid ending up with my own idea of God, I must bring all these strands and thoughts together and hold them up beside what God has actually said about himself. Just as I cannot come to a deep knowledge of another person merely by watching them, I have one day to let them speak to me, so it is with God – I must let him tell me his story, I must begin to read his word. This is where we shall need the help of someone who is wise, not clever, someone who has searched, listened, formed pictures and had eventually to discard them.

What method we use for reading God's word is up to us. Some people go systematically through a book, while others follow the Church's readings and thus keep in tune with the liturgical seasons. Some use books where texts are commented on like *Every Day With Jesus*, written by Selwyn Hughes and published by the Crusade for World Revival, or *The Word Among Us* published by Turvey Abbey in Bedfordshire. The latter publication takes the readings from the daily liturgical celebration of the Roman Catholic Church. Some people prefer more detailed commentaries like those of William Barclay. We need to find what suits us. What is important is that we do not become flibbertigibbets, following no system, just going here and there.

Juan Carlos Ortiz, a Pentecostal minister from South America, said in his book *Disciple* that we ought not to underline our favourite passages in Scripture. I was surprised to read this because I had found it helpful to highlight certain passages. But the point he was making was valid – he was suggesting that we might end up only reading our favourite passages and never reading the whole word. When we begin to realise just how much God loves and cares for us, then we will be anxious to hear *all* of his word, no matter what it says to us, for we will be beginning to trust in him.

Growth

When Jesus promised to send us the Holy Spirit he said that the Spirit would 'lead' us into truth. We are not meant to get a totally passive idea that willy-nilly we will be blindly led. We have to search, look, question, agonise over – confident that all our stumblings are growth points. When God makes plants grow, he does not just give them growth, but rather he causes many complicated processes to take place within the plant and these then result in growth. So too it is with us; he uses our very activity, our searchings, even our despairs to bring us to that point where we say: 'Into your hands I commend my spirit.'

Each journey is unique. My own troubled journey brought me to the place where I had to dare to believe that the God I was hearing about was really good. This meant having to undo false impressions, and what a battle that was. It is so easy to allow bad habits of thinking to persist. Once we have begun to see that our thoughts of God are wrong, we must wage war against them, and ask God's forgiveness when we, time and time again, let falsehood lead us. Only as I began to change my internal idea of God did I find a thirst growing in me to hear what this true God had to say to me. And as I looked at words that had often frightened me, I began to see how I had misunderstood them because of the wrong image I had about the One who stood behind those words. Perhaps this is what Isaiah was talking about when he said:

You will listen and listen again, but not
  understand, see and see again, but not
  perceive.
For the heart of this nation has grown
  coarse,
their ears are dull of hearing, and they have
  shut their eyes,
for fear they should see with their eyes,
hear with their ears,
understand with their heart,

and be converted and be healed by me.
(quoted Matt. 13:14–15)

How important it is to make sure that our idea of God does resemble in some way the picture he has given us of himself. In this image of God, evil must not have its place. We must constantly revamp our ideas, knowing that no picture can capture him. Today we are learning how harmful certain foods can be; they may look attractive, even taste good, but in time their true value shows. It is the same with what we let into our minds. If I allow myself to have false ideas about God, then I will grow suspicious of him and begin to mistrust his promises. Satan could not be more delighted with such a disaster.

This is why we must seek to know God fully. We must search for him in the world around us, the world within us and in our fellow human beings. But also we must listen to what this God has told us, because what he has shared with us could never have been dreamed up by one of us; it is too magnificent, too marvellous. Our knowledge of God's word must go further than quoting: 'Thou shalt not . . .' We need to hear what this our God has done for us and we need the courage to dare to believe what he has done, what he has most surely done.

That is why there is a battle for our mind, for if we can be persuaded not to believe, then the new life won for us with such sweat and

84

pain will never come to flower, and our lives, even though they may be respectable and decent, will not be powerful and earth-shaking; they will just be nice, and we are called to be more than that.

6

Prayer: A Calling to Mind

Hear, O Israel: the Lord our God is one Lord; and you shall love the Lord your God with all your heart, and with all your soul, and with all your might. And these words which I command you this day shall be upon your heart; you shall teach them diligently to your children, and you shall talk of them when you sit in your house, and when you walk by the way, and when you lie down and when you rise. (Deut. 6:4–7) (Roman Missal)

If you want to get a sun-tan, you have to get into the sunshine. Getting into the sunshine may be very costly, it may require a lot of organisation and effort, it may entail over-coming many problems. However, the cost, the efforts and the overcoming of problems do not tan you; they only get you into the place where the sun can tan you. If you want to be holy, then you have to get into the place where God can make you holy. The place where God can make you holy is the place of faith; the place where we acknowledge and accept what God has done for us through the death and resurrection of his Son. Getting into that place requires much discipline, much hard work and there will be many difficulties to be surmounted; but the discipline, the hard work and the surmounting of the problems do not make you holy, they only get you into the place where God can work on you.

While the above analogy is helpful, the parallels break down in the last part. Sunbathing is a very passive occupation. All you have to do is sit or lie in the sun, and the sun does all the work. On the other hand standing in the place of faith requires constant acknowledging, constant accepting of God's truth. God's truth is not true because we feel it to be so, nor does it always appeal to our reason. It is true because God says it is. To keep standing in this truth involves much effort and discipline. Faith is action, it is not passive mental acceptance. The way we live changes because of what we believe. For me, prayer is standing in that place of faith.

Prayer is a subject that is vast and wide, and many people have written about it. The number of books on prayer is astounding, and in this chapter I am not really seeking to add to this enormous library. I want to say what I have found helpful. I think it is important to pray in the way you find *you* can pray. Do not go adopting other people's methods for the sake of it. If it is helpful, fine, use it and do not be

afraid to adapt it. If it is not helpful, then drop
it. Prayer is very personal for it is a relating to
God. We all relate in our own unique way and
that is why I say: pray as *you* can.

Many of us learnt of prayer as petition. 'If
you want something, well, ask God for it.'
Certainly prayer includes petitions, but they are
only part of it. Imagine a relationship that only
knew petition! 'Get me this. Come here. Find
that. Put this there.' I do not think it would
last very long. Relationships require sharings,
tellings, listenings, ponderings, and sometimes
just being together.

I do not know when I began to think of
prayer as a dialogue and not as a monologue.
I suppose the monologue idea stemmed from
imagining that God does not speak to us. It is
the word 'speak' that puts most people off. It
sounds too personal, too direct. Yet Jesus said:
'I will send my Spirit to you and he will lead
you into the complete truth' (John 16:8–13) –
that is pretty personal and direct. In the first
book of Samuel (3:1–9) we are told how the
boy Samuel thought he heard the high priest
Eli calling him. Three times he went to Eli, and
three times Eli told him that he had not called
him. The last time Eli said this to Samuel he
added: 'If you hear that voice again, say:
"Speak, Lord, your servant is listening".' This,
I think, is a good recipe for prayer. Listen for
the Lord, and then respond to him. Alas, so
often our prayer is: 'Listen, Lord, for your

servant is speaking.' In the last chapter we looked at the various ways that God speaks to us.

So, for me, prayer is going very deliberately into that place of faith where I take what God has said and I respond to it. That is why it is important during the day to have our antennae out, ready to catch God's messages in whatever way they come. We need to remember them. Sometimes just jotting down a phrase on a bit of paper is enough to trigger off the memory as we come into that place of faith.

I think it is important to hear God in all the ways he communicates with us. If I only listen to the God of creation, discovering his might, his power, his beauty, I will miss his work of redemption. There is so much more to God than his role as creator, great and marvellous as that is. God is in the cities and in the slums, but not all of us can readily have the privilege of seeing him in nature. Besides, there is a natural search for transcendence in all of us, and we could so easily end up by feeding on vague, misty sentiments, deluding ourselves that we are mystics. Prayer is very *practical*. It is not waltzing in the clouds. To know someone we need to know the whole of them. If we just know what they do, and have never heard them speak, then we do not know them. The same is true when I just know what someone says, and yet have never seen them do anything. I meet people who know God as creator, but do not seem to know him as redeemer. I also meet people who know the redeeming God, but do not seem to know him as the creator God. I find great richness in true ecumenical discussions, for we all look at the same God in slightly different ways.

So, quite simply, when I pray I deliberately call to mind what God may have said in a whole variety of ways and respond to it. When I am deaf to his messages, then I have nothing to respond to, and prayer becomes dry and heavy.

We can learn a great deal by looking at the way the Church prays. She is always responding to God's love and mercy. Take, for example, the hymn from Morning Prayer for Sunday of the first week in the Roman breviary:

Transcendent God in whom we live
The resurrection and the Light,
We sing to you a morning hymn
To end the silence of the night.

When early cock begins to crow
and everything from sleep awakes,
New life and hope spring up again
While out of darkness colour breaks.

Creator of all things that are,,
The measure and the end of all,
Forgiving God forget our sins,
And hear our prayer before we call.

Praise Father, Son and Holy Ghost,
Blest Trinity and source of grace,

Who calls us out of nothingness
To find in you our resting-place.

'While out of darkness colour breaks' – what a
beautiful way of describing the dawn! The
Church makes much use of the psalms for her
prayers. In Psalm 136 there is the constant
refrain: 'His steadfast love endures for ever.'
While the singer of the psalm declares that God
is good, God is supreme, God is Lord, this
refrain keeps on being repeated. Adding our
own appreciation of God to the list from the
psalm, we can learn how to pray.

Meditation and contemplation

Before looking at the practical way that I try
to put myself into that place of faith and
respond, I would like to say something about
meditation and contemplation. Modern man is
distracted and scattered. So many demands are
made on us that we become over-stimulated.
We are called this way and that; we become
divided in ourselves, bombarded by music,
lights, smells. Countless things are vying for our
attention. It is not surprising that when we
settle down to pray, we find ourselves full of
competing thoughts. Our mind is in a whirl,
and it is nearly impossible to be still. We could
try and conquer this problem by spending all
our prayer time in 'said' prayer. At least we
would feel that we are filling the time with

prayer. But 'said' prayers can often just be that – said and not prayed. More importantly we then give no time to listening.

Today I meet many people from different Christian backgrounds, and they are searching for new ways to pray, for deeper ways to encounter God. How wonderful it is that we are all beginning to seek the riches in the different denominations. There seems to be a thirst to know something about the prayer of quiet. Many have tried to be still, to concentrate their thoughts on one subject, but have found their minds just too active, and so they have wrongly thought that this sort of prayer is only for certain people. Everyone, I believe, should be able to experience something of the prayer of quiet. I admit this field is a little confusing, because the words 'meditate' and 'contemplate' are used differently by different people. So a brief word to help clarify them.

Strictly speaking 'meditation' is a purely human technique. It can be used to help a person pray, but in itself it is not prayer. Because we live such scattered lives, we are often unaware of how unaware we are. Meditation is a skill to help us become aware, especially of the present moment. It is useful for all sorts of reasons, and some business firms even look for 'meditators' because they are more alert. Meditation can also help us pray. For example, most of us are quite oblivious to the various parts of our bodies; that is why meditating exercises make us concentrate on one part of our body to make us aware of our unawareness. Unconsciously we breathe. When we start thinking about this we notice that we can control our breathing, we can do it quickly or deeply, we can even stop doing it for a short time, but normally we just breathe. Most of us are unconscious of our feet, unless they are hurting, or of our back, our neck. We are also unconscious of the sounds around us, the colours, the light. Meditating makes us more fully alive to the present moment. It is a gathering of our scattered self into one. It only becomes prayer when I begin to ask: 'Who makes me breathe? Who invented sound, colour? What is he saying to me through all these things? Who gave me the various parts to my body?' It is a seeing of God here and now, not lost in some far distant history, and we respond to his touch with love and gratitude.

In this place of quiet we are better disposed to hear the God who is forever approaching us. Because my being is not stirred and filled up with many things, I can more easily recognise him. How wonderful it is to realise that my life is something that I receive minute by minute. Naturally I must take care of it, but it is not mine in the sense that I make it. Seeing life as a gift can alter the way we live, and how lovely it is to meet grateful people. Such awareness can help us to carry God into every experience of life, and this makes us more and more conscious of him speaking to us in the ordinary things. In this way we can begin to replace our wrong ideas of God with truer ones. It may have to be done painstakingly at first, but slowly the lies will give way to the truth. Scripture tells us to 'pray without ceasing' (1 Thess. 5:17). Prayer means relating and when we relate with God at every moment of the day, we are praying without ceasing.

When talking about the purely Christian variety, meditation tends to refer to when we actively engage ourselves in picturing and pondering a gospel scene, even imagining ourselves present, so as to enter more fully into the teachings. Contemplation, on the other hand, is more passive, the activity being God's rather than our own.

Unfortunately there is an aura attached to contemplative prayer. Many think it is only for special people, and they fight shy of it, and thus close themselves off to God's gift. Others, thinking it is a higher form of prayer, are anxious to be in 'club class', and they can get lost in all sorts of 'mystic' experiences which are more of the flesh than of the spirit. No idea we have of God *is* God. When we begin to realise that, we cease trying to picture him. We begin to rest in his presence. We are not too bothered how he is present, we just know he is. We cannot force this to happen in ourselves. It comes from the heart, not from our decision. It is abandoning ourselves to a God whom we really do not know, but it is done with utmost trust; and it is this abandoning that I would call contemplative prayer. Getting to be in relationship with God in this way is to set out on a journey, an exploration, a great search. The quest never finishes, you never arrive. Fr Cyprian Smith OSB, who wrote *The Way of Paradox*, said once in a talk: 'There are no gurus, no experts, we are all still searching. All we can do is share our travel notes.'

It is beyond the scope of this book to enter deeply into the field of meditation and contemplation. There are many books on the whole area, but before you plunge into reading widely you ought to find out something about the standpoint an author is writing from, perhaps by asking the advice of a friend. I know of some Christians who went to join a 'meditation group' and discovered it had little to do with what they understood meditation to be.

My own experience of prayer

Prayer has, for most people, a certain fascination. We love to read about it, we love to talk about it, but often this can be a stalling, a putting off getting down to actual prayer. What other people write about prayer seems enticing and we would like to experience the same. But often our experience is not like that and we tend to give up, or go and buy more books on prayer, and again fail to get down to it. I want now to speak about the practical steps I take in trying to pray. Remember: pray as *you* can, do not adopt what is not helpful to you.

Being a monk I am lucky, for built into our life there are times for prayer. Besides the office, which we say in common, we must all have our time for personal prayer with the Lord. Because my life is fairly regular, it is easy to find a fixed time for quiet prayer. For most people this is difficult. We live in a very hectic world and I know just how busy many of my friends are. But I think we have to be very firm about this. When there is something that we really want to do, we can usually make time for it. After all who gave us time? Surely it is right that we find some to be with God. A fixed time is helpful; if we leave it to chance, we will discover that prayer gets crowded out.

It is also good to have a place where you pray. Again we monks are spoilt. Finding a place in a house where there are small children can really be a problem. But I see married couples achieving this, the husband taking on the chores while the wife escapes for a time, and then the wife letting the husband go off before the Lord.

When I began to take prayer more seriously, that is, to say more than morning and night prayers, I did not really know what to do. I used to try to think about God and say something to him. This was not easy because being unable to visualise him I found I could not keep my attention on him. After a while I used to focus on Jesus because I could at least have some picture of him. When I was in a religious mood, this worked reasonably well, but I was not often in such a mood. Also once I had got my mind on to Jesus, I had the problem of not knowing what to say. I could not have an ordinary conversation, because he knew everything already, so it became rather natural to ask my requests. I read, and heard about, people being silent in prayer, but I discovered that I could not handle silences. Either I was soon off down some alley of distraction or I fell asleep. I tried visualising scenes from the Gospels, but I could never get much from that. I certainly never expected to hear God speak, though I think after reading some book that I did hope for a while. I tried listening but most times I heard absolutely nothing, or if I did think of something I was never sure if it was God or me that I was hearing. I came to the conclusion that God only spoke to his saints and so I gave up listening.

A time came when, through my ecumenical activities, I began to meet people who often said, 'God told me' or 'I really didn't know what to do, so I prayed and then I just knew'. I was highly suspicious and thoroughly put off. It was not my experience, but since some of the people who said this were men and women I really respected, I began to pursue this idea of God speaking. Thank God for good, wise friends who told me to read Scriptures and start listening to what God *has* said, before straining to hear what he *is saying*. This was not a very great success because the image I already had of God prevented me from really hearing the good news. Every time Jesus said some hard saying, I felt guilty; and somehow when he said a merciful thing, I could not apply it to myself. Again it was good friends who made me take authority over this situation. They taught me to discipline my thoughts. They showed me how I was living on my feelings and not on the truth. Scripture was true, whether I felt it to be so or not. I was not even asked to understand why, I was simply asked to accept the word of God as the truth. So I began taking central parts of the gospel, and I stated them to myself imagining that God was saying this or that truth to me. I then began to thank him for it and to praise him and bless him. It was by no means easy, but in some way I felt I knew what I should do even though I found it hard. I started to see how important it is to be on the look-out for phrases in Scripture or moments of insight during the day, and to treasure these and bring them to mind when I pray. Since God is always communicating with us, I will hear him if I am alert; but if I have not looked for him, I will have missed him. I am reminded of T. S. Eliot's poem 'Little Gidding' (my italics):

At the source of the longest river
The voice of the hidden waterfall
And the children in the apple-tree
Not known, because not looked for
But heard, half-heard, in the stillness
Between two waves of the sea.

How important it is to be awake to the present moment.

I try to make this calling to mind of some basic truth a very real act. It is so easy to go through motions. When the psalmist tells us to 'sing a new song', I do not think it means we are to find a brand new song; rather we are to sing something we know but do it as though we have never sung it before. I find, as time goes on, that even though I am recalling a well-known truth, it often comes to mind as though it was new. If I am alone, I will speak out my gratitude and praise. I do not try to work up my feelings. I simply thank God for what he has done. Some days it is easier than others, but on the hard days I have a sense that what I am about is the most important thing I can do. When we praise God, we put him in the centre, and that is a healthy thing to do. It is hard because we like to be in the centre, that is why praise is so difficult. It truly is a sacrifice. The truths that I praise God for have, over the months, become very real. I seem to have grown in understanding of their spiritual content. For me now, the death and resurrec-

tion of Jesus Christ are things of central importance. I had always been told they were
important and I had accepted that, but now I
know for myself how vital they are. I think
this has come about because I have spent time
thanking God for his Son's death and resurrection even though I did not view them as top
truths.

I am beginning to see a difference between
understanding a truth because I have worked
at it with my mind, and suddenly grasping the
meaning of something when there has been no
real work on my part. When I use my mind I
get to an answer through a logical process, but
when I have a flash of enlightenment I just
know and I am not too certain why I know. In
the Roman Missal in the preface for the first
week of Lent, there is this beautiful statement:
'Whenever we call to mind the great events that
gave us new life in Christ, You (Father) bring
the image of Your Son to perfection within us.'
In other words, when we bless God for the
work he has done through his Son, we are transformed into Christ and begin to know spiritual
truths with a new mind.

It is difficult to explain exactly what happens
during my prayer time because it is a very personal time. If I sink into mooning, then I have
to stir myself and get to work. Sometimes I ask
God questions, and I am now beginning to be
confident that he will answer although maybe
not immediately. Very often I wait months

before I get some light. Some days ideas flow quite well, and in order not to lose them, I always have a notebook at hand to jot down, very briefly, what was helpful. It is interesting reading over those jottings after a month or so and seeing how themes develop.

My biggest temptation is to get excited about insights and just go over them again and again in my mind. I fear I am often delighting more in the fact that I have had an insight than in what I have seen. We can get chuffed with ourselves, and fail to notice the goodness of God in revealing something to us. When I discover this I simply ask God's forgiveness and try to turn my failure to God's profit by being amazed that he still bothers with me.

Another temptation is to cut the time short; this usually happens on the days when I am trying deliberately to praise God. I can get consumed with a desire to be up and doing something. On those days, time drags and five minutes can seem like half an hour. It is humiliating to realise that at such times I am really saying to God: 'I find you dull, and I would much prefer to be about my own business.' I know that sentiment is not really true – it is more of a feeling than a reality – but even so I ask God's forgiveness for it and beg him to change it for I cannot do so myself.

Some days I am quite vocal, putting my praise into words; other days I am silent. Not silent with emptiness, silent because I cannot find words. The more I pray, the more I become aware of my sinfulness – not so much sinful actions, though of course those still persist, but rather an understanding of how self-centred I still am in spite of God's graces. All these discoveries do not flatter us, but then we do not pray to have ourselves flattered. I suppose it stands to reason that the nearer we approach God, the more we are going to notice the blemishes in ourselves. God does not reveal these to humiliate us; he does it so that we will honestly confess them and then experience the truth that his Son has borne them for us.

In prayer we undertake a vast journey from self to God. It is a journey that we cannot accomplish by our own efforts. We may start praying for very selfish motives, we may be looking for consolations, the satisfaction of being thought holy, an insurance policy for a happy hereafter – God in his mercy is very patient. He spoils us with consolations and joy. In time, though, he begins to prune, and prayer becomes dull and heavy. Alas, most give up at this moment. It really is a moment for growth. And so we need to know about the seasons of prayer, the good times and the difficult.

Dryness in prayer

When we notice that our prayer has dried up, become routine and dull, our first reaction ought to be to look at our lives. Has something gone wrong, a bad relationship grown up, or is there some unrepented fault? All these things can cause a clouding in our prayer life. Care must be taken that as we examine ourselves we do not become over-scrupulous, for none of us is perfect. What we are looking for is some new and recent fault. When nothing obvious can be found, and if the dryness continues, then it may be that God is purifying us. The trouble is that if prayer is always found to be rewarding, then, we could so easily do it just for that. So, God may have to dry things up a bit, to make us ask the question: 'Am I here for me or for him?'

There are both little nights, which are quickly over, and winter seasons, which can endure for very long periods. During these periods we need a wise companion, and they are not always easily found. This experience of a long, dry patch can be extremely painful, and there seems to be no good got from it. It is one thing to pray to a God who does not appear to be listening, but it is quite something else to pray to a God whom you no longer think exists. I know when I went through a very lengthy dry period, it seemed impossible to convey to anyone the agony I experienced. The people I found the most helpful were those who just stood with me in my doubts and did not argue. No number of doubts add up to an unbelief. It is not wrong to doubt, question, ponder – all that is part of the journey of faith, but there is a terrible loneliness when one stands in a place where others never seem to pass.

When prayer is dry, that is the time when methods, plans, schemes can be useful. Words taken from a familiar prayer, for example the Lord's Prayer, can be thoughtfully gone through. Do not judge your prayer by what you get out of it, rather look at how much you put into it. The very fact that you give time, you stay there, even though you are empty, is a good sign. Imagine visiting a sick person only because you enjoyed it.

Prayer is this vast journey from where self is centre to where God is centre. Such a journey is bound to be painful. We can deceive ourselves and imagine that we have put God in the centre, when all the time we are admiring ourselves for putting God in the centre. When prayer is empty, and yet we still continue with it, then at least we are beginning not to be there for our own comfort. These barren periods are necessary and God knows when best to send them. They prove to be great growth points.

A Sure Foundation: Concluding Thoughts

Therefore, everyone who listens to these words of mine and acts on them will be like a sensible man who built his house on rock. Rain came down, floods rose, gales blew and hurled themselves against that house, and it did not fall: it was founded on rock. (Matt. 7:25)

Living in the Spirit is not to live by holy nudges. God certainly can and does nudge us, but from the way some people talk you would imagine that the Holy Spirit sits on their shoulders directing their every move. That God could do this, I have no doubt; but that God would do this, I doubt very much, save on rare occasions.

To live by the Spirit is first to know what the Spirit came to reveal. Secondly, it is to believe what the Spirit reveals. Thirdly, it is to keep in mind what the Spirit reveals. One of the main problems facing the Church is, I think, the ignorance that so many Christians have about the central message of the gospel. The gospel covers many important topics, and different ones can be adopted by different people as their favourite; in doing this it is so easy for the main message to get marginalised and for it to lose its significance as a life-giving truth. The central point of the gospel is that Jesus died for our sins and rose to new life. In dying he paid the consequences for our sins, and because, as God, any action of his had infinite value, the result of sin, a blockage between humanity and God, has been removed. This means that it is possible for people to be in relationship again with God; but each individual has to accept what God has done, and how God has done it. Senior citizens now have all sorts of benefits available to them, but they have to prove that they are senior citizens; so, too, we have to prove we are eligible to receive what Christ has done for us, and we do that by submitting our sins, and confessing that Jesus, through his death, has paid for those sins.

That is not all: there is more to this basic truth. Death could not keep hold of Jesus, the innocent man, and on his resurrection, he became the new man. Here was someone over whom evil had no power. This work of Jesus was not just to remove the barrier caused by sin, it was to take away the very sinfulness of man by giving him a new life. Life is not just something we have, like a suitcase, which we keep in the attic and use from time to time; no, it is something that we must always use. We live life, we do not just have it. So, too, with this new life; it is not just something we have, it is something we need constantly to use. In order to do this, we daily, hourly have to remind ourselves that, with Christ, we are dead in our old life and are alive with his new life. It is this conscious, daily decision to live in that place of faith, that enables us to know the power of the risen Lord. Every thought or anxiety that threatens to cast us into gloom or insecurity must be firmly grasped and expelled. As we find again and again that place of peace, we will experience the truth of the words: 'I am the Way . . . no one can come to the Father save through me' (John 14:6). It is not that all problems will fade away, we may well have to go right through the centre of the storm, but there comes an inner certainty that we cannot be snatched out of the hand of God.

The difficulty that I meet as I try to counsel and help people stems from their distorted idea of God and his word. Having suffered from this myself, I know how effective it can be in numbing the power of the gospel to set one free. Imagine what it feels like to be told that Christianity is the answer to the mystery of life, and yet not experience that as true! It puts you in a terrible spot. You are told 'this is the truth', and because you do not experience it as true, you feel guilty, isolated, alone. You may not have the guts to abandon it completely, after all there are some terrible threats attached to leaving, and so you settle for being a misfit, and you cover up, putting a good face on it all.

I really understand the bitterness and resentments that some Christians carry around buried deep within their being. All these hurts can have different effects – some people become belligerent and hostile, others turn in on themselves and end up insecure, fearful, oversubmissive, full of self-reproach.

In this book I have tried to make you look at who God is for you. It is so easy to answer the party line and deceive ourselves. For years I would never admit my inmost feelings about God, not so much because I was ashamed of them, but because I did not really know they were there. These inmost thoughts need exposing to the light; we must hold them up to God's own revelation of himself and be honest about what we see. As I have said before, we would be greatly helped by having some wise, not clever, person to be a sounding board.

I have also tried to spell out the wound that is in us and to look at what God has told us about its origin. This, I know, is walking into a thorny area, which could easily deflect us from trying to hear what God is saying. I suppose it is not surprising that we should find such difficulty in accepting responsibility for something which we did not actually do. If we are honest we will find an inner resentment, but that reaction is the very symptom of what has gone wrong. We are looking at things from our point of view and not from God's. If you have a camera with the viewfinder out of line with the lens, although you may focus your viewfinder on what you wish to photograph, in fact your lens is focused on something else. We were made for God, and we centre on self, and what is worse when we think we are centering on God, often we are fixed on ourselves. Because of the wound deep within us, we find it very difficult to look at things save from our own point of view. We much prefer to argue our case, and thus put off that moment of confessing.

We have the same trouble over the salvation won for us by Jesus Christ. It is very difficult to be on the receiving end. Our whole western education teaches us to be self-sufficient, and so it is very natural that we should take that over into religion – we want some credit for being saved. We can argue that it has been no easy task to remain faithful, we may list the sacrifices, tot up the cost, but the fact remains that you cannot win eternal life. Eternal life is God-life. There is nothing a creature could do to merit God-life. A good ape could never merit human life. Besides Jesus never said that following him would be easy. Our self-loving being will resist all the way while God works his transformation in us. We will certainly be rewarded in heaven for the good we do, but good works cannot merit eternal life, which we need for entering heaven in the first place.

To be hazy about these central truths is to cut at the very heart of the gospel. Anything that can divert us from life-giving truth and make us occupied with some other truth, even though important, can successfully keep us from the power of the gospel. What is worse, we can stay within the ranks of the Church, and yet somehow never be fully Church, because to be ignorant about what God has done for us in Christ Jesus virtually means that we do not have faith in his saving work. It is faith in that truth that gives life.

Ignorance about what God has done is serious, but it is not enough to know what he has done, we need to believe it. Here again we can mistake intellectual assent for faith. Faith has to be demonstrated in action, and by action I do not just mean good works. I mean living my daily life according to what I profess to believe. If I live full of fear of God, anxious with regard to my salvation, I am demonstrating that I do not trust in the saving work of Jesus Christ and still basically rely on my own performance. I do believe also that as we allow the new life of Christ to develop in us, we will do the good deeds that have been commanded us: 'We are God's work of art, created in Christ Jesus to live the good life as from the beginning he meant us to live it' (Ephesians 2:10). The sad thing is that we can set out to do great good but in our own power: 'it is the spirit that gives life, the flesh has nothing to offer' (John 6:63). If we boast that we have the life of Christ in us and yet never

110

give any indication by our action that this is so, then the absence of fruit makes others question the truth of what we say. Our belief is betrayed by our actions.

We are asked to believe that through the death and rising of Jesus our sins have been dealt with and that we have received a new life to enable us to live in a new way. Once upon a time that truth, though never actually denied, was not central in my life. Christianity for me was behaving in a morally acceptable way. It was up to me to get my life into shape. I became what I now call a 'muscular Christian'. I gritted my teeth and did my best. Results followed: I learnt to smile when I was angry, I could keep a reasonable exterior calm when I was impatient. But that was the trouble – it was only external. Later when I began to learn the truth about Christ's death and resurrection, I did not find that I applied what I knew to my living. I remained the muscular monk. For a long time I was not conscious of this dichotomy; but as I began to be aware of it, I was puzzled as to how to apply the truth that through the cross of Jesus I was saved. Did this mean I just waited until the power of God set me free? Just what was I meant to do? I think this is a good example of how our darkened mind works. I was suffering from a spiritual blindness – it all seemed nonsense to me, although I knew deep down that it was not right to just sit around until the saving power came upon me. I had to do something, but that something was not to continue with my muscular efforts.

In time I began to see that my efforts were to be channelled into fervent acts of faith in the cross of Jesus. I had to praise God deliberately for what he had achieved through Christ. The change was not sudden, but gradually I began to see that habits which had held me in their grip did not seem to be so dominant. While I was spending this time praising and thanking God, I did of course do my best to control my life – but I now knew these efforts of mine were not the solution. They, in a sense, were the best I could do, until the Lord had mercy on me and made his Son's work effective in me. Remember the example I gave about rowing or sailing a boat. When you row a boat, it is your effort that moves it; when you sail a boat, it is the wind that moves it, but you have a lot to do. You do not just sit there, you cooperate with the power of the wind.

To believe is to act out the truth that you know. The devil knows the truth, but it has not helped him because he refuses to accept it. To be able continually to act out this truth we must constantly call it to mind. Because of the way we have been brought up, because of what we have learnt or picked up unconsciously from life, our ways of thinking need changing. We have fallen into patterns of thought that come from the world and not from the Spirit. Someone said that religion is not taught, it is caught. There is some truth in that, for gospel truths can be passed on to us and they come to be part of what we know, but do not become a life-giving experience. There is all the difference in the world between knowing about someone – I can be taught that – and knowing someone, which only happens through direct contact. It is the Holy Spirit who provides us with that direct contact. Scripture, without the aid of the Spirit, can fail to introduce us to the real Jesus. I have met too many people who even after honest searching in Scripture have failed to meet the true Christ. They have confessed to me that the Jesus they met they did not find warm and approachable. I am convinced that they were bringing into their thinking some very early impression that they had of him. He was for them, and alas for so many, the pale Galilean who was very correct and always right, but rather forbidding. I can remember reading on a church hall board a sign which said, 'God is watching'.

Hence our patterns of thought need careful examination – are we allowing wrong and false pictures to colour our thinking, thus affecting our every encounter with Christ? To be able to control this habit, we need to spend time consciously and deliberately calling to mind the great events that gave us new life in Christ, and then praising and thanking God for his great love and mercy. This is not magic, it is not a matter of just saying formulas of belief; what is required is a deep, convinced faith. Faith is a gift, and we must continually ask for it and exercise it. This exercise is what I call prayer: a deliberate responding to God's revelation. In prayer we remind ourselves of God's plan and check how much we live by that. We must not be like the man in the Letter of James (1:22–5) who looked into the mirror and then went away and forgot what he had seen. There are powerful forces working to make us forget the central message.

I see prayer as the continual dialogue in which God reminds us of all he has done, and we, in accepting and consenting to this, experience its power to change our lives. Quite simply we need to know what God has done for us, believe in its efficacy and continually keep it in mind as we walk through life. As we obey God's word already spoken, we will begin to realise it is actually being spoken to us, and thus we will be open to hear the God who does speak to us his personal word.

Jesus was also led by the Holy Spirit

Jesus, himself, was led by the Spirit and at first there must have been a growing excitement in him as he saw more clearly his role and his Father backing his words with signs and wonders. This enthusiasm would have been caught by his own disciples and by the crowds as they saw that Jesus fitted their picture of the expected Messiah. 'Here is the one who was promised. With such power and miracles, he will surely deliver us from all our foes' – these and similar words would have spread like wildfire among the people.

But a time came when Jesus changed. He became more mysterious. Even before the transfiguration, he began to hint that he was to die. After the experience on the mountain, he set his face towards Jerusalem and seemed determined to go there even though he foretold that he would be arrested and killed. What happened on that mountain? Did Moses and Elijah speak with him about his passing? The face of Jesus shone, not as though a light was shining on him, but as though a light was shining out from him. Was he receiving an inner illumination about the Father's will for him? Was he seeing clearly what the Father was asking? This would account for his changed attitude after the vision and why he began instructing his disciples about his passing: 'He was telling them, "The Son of Man will be delivered into the hands of men; they will put him to death; and three days after he has been put to death he will rise again". But they did not understand what he said and were afraid to ask him' (Mark 9:31–2). I am not saying that Jesus did not know until then what he was destined for. Before the transfiguration he had rounded on Peter when he tried to turn him away from his foretold death. We read in Scrip-

ture that Jesus grew in wisdom and knowledge,
and I feel that on the mountain he gained clarification about his future, and thus on coming
down he determined to go to Jerusalem and the
mode of his life changed.

I am forever speculating about how much
Jesus knew. As God, of course, he would know
everything. Did that knowledge affect his
human knowledge? I have no idea; that is the
sort of question theologians like to grapple
with. I tend to side with those who say that
his human knowledge was incomplete. I find
comfort in thinking of him also in the dark,
following blindly the Father's will. What was
asked of him was so opposite to fulfilling the
role of liberator. He was asked to fail, to be
conquered, to be hounded out of the city and
to die as a criminal. Could he see through all
that to the victory to follow? It is difficult to
tell. I find it good to wrestle with such questions, and in prayer to ask the Lord to enlighten
me. The point I want to make here is what
happened to the Master will surely happen to
the disciple; we, too, will suffer hardship, and
perhaps for no apparent reason.

Teilhard de Chardin in *Le Milieu Divin* talks
of a time of positive growth and development,
and he sees that as an essential part of one's
life; but he also talks of a time of diminishment,
and this for the sake of being in another. I
regret that the gospel came to me first as
diminishment. I heard about giving up,

renouncing, dying, before I had heard, 'Be fruitful, multiply, fill the earth and conquer it' (Genesis 1:28). God certainly does prune, but if there has been no growth, how can he prune? Also if I do not experience the hand that prunes as first loving and tender, then how can I trust when the time for cutting back arrives? Jesus had perfect confidence in his Father. He who loved the lilies of the field and talked about such homely things as harvest, grape growing, fishing, must have delighted in this world and forever have seen traces of his Father. Thus when the Father revealed his deep plan, Jesus was anxious to fulfil it no matter how strange it may have appeared.

'I will send my Spirit to you and he will lead you into the complete truth' (John 16:13). That promise is made to every one of us, and we need to allow the Spirit to challenge us over our ideas of God; we must be forever growing, seeing things in new and deeper ways. Not only is the Spirit in us, we also have the Lord who walked in trust of his Father living in us, and he promised:

> If anyone loves me he will keep my word,
> and my Father will love him,
> and we shall come to him
> and make our home with him. (John 14:23)

To walk in the way of the spirit, without the directing of the Holy Spirit, runs the very real risk of being led off down a labyrinth of ways, enticing, appealing, but alas a subtle self-centred search into our natural yen for mysticism. We are seeking after God, not mysticism. This quest requires discipline, determination and guidance. But when all is said and done, we find in the end that what we fondly thought was our search for God, was really his search for us and much of our striving has been our refusal to be found by him.

'Not my will, but yours' – how difficult it is to move from an attitude of heroic sacrifice to one of convinced, joyful surrender, and to discover yet again, it was not our achievement but his achieving in us.